Prepare to Win

LESSONS LEARNED AT
KNIGHT
SCHOOL

Compiled & Edited by David Skibinski with Bob Hammel

Published & distributed by:

David Skibinski

in association with:

IBJ Book Publishing

41 E. Washington St., Suite 200

Indianapolis, IN 46204

www.ibjbp.com

Library of Congress Control Number: 2013921368

ISBN 978-1-939550-00-2

First Edition

Printed in the United States of America

Contents

Introduction

From 1976-1980 I had the distinct pleasure of serving as a basketball manager for Coach Bob Knight at Indiana University. We were fortunate to win the NIT Championship in 1979 and Big Ten Championship in 1980; unfortunately for me it was right between the NCAA National Championships in 1976 and 1981. I was also fortunate to have tremendous classmates on the team including Michael Woodson, Glen Grunwald and Butch Carter, and fellow manager classmates Pete Schroeder, Chris Stone and John Levenda. We shared a great four years together and I will cherish those memories forever.

In the summer of 2008, newly appointed Indiana University Basketball Coach Tom Crean, with support from Cook and Company, hosted a reunion of ALL former IU Basketball players, coaches, managers and staff. It was a fabulous gathering at West Baden, Indiana that saw numerous generations of the Indiana University Basketball family come together to re-establish the foundation of Indiana Basketball. I enjoyed the opportunity to meet many of the men that built the tradition of Indiana Basketball.

Of course, it was great to see so many of the players from my years (1976-1980) at Indiana as a basketball manager: Kent Benson, Wayne Radford, Chuck Franz and more. But what made the event invigorating was meeting not only the managers with whom I worked at Indiana, but many of those who held that same position before and after my time. As we all got acquainted, it was fun to recall the good times we had, and how similar some of the stories were for those of us who worked behind the scenes at Assembly Hall with and for Coach Knight.

One thing was evident as I listened to the stories being told, collectively, we were a successful group of men. Many of us had gone on to become educators and coaches, while others were doing well in business, law and medicine. Across the board we were all successful in our chosen field, and we all looked back on our experiences working for Coach Knight as formative and fun. I was delighted to hear the stories of the lessons we all seemed to have learned from Coach, and how those lessons were still in practice for all of us today.

During Coach Knight's career at Indiana more than 100 young college students served on his staff as managers. The common perception of a basketball manager is that of a "water boy," but our experience was one of responsibility and contribution to our collective success as a team. Our staff worked on the court during drills, put players through shooting drills before and after practice, blew the whistle as referees during scrimmages, managed road trips, filmed practice, edited game film into highlight reels for Coach Knight, and much, much more. And, like the players, we listened, intently, when "the man" spoke; like the players, we carried notebooks and made notes; like the players, we "water boys" learned to compete like elite basketball champions.

While many books have been written about Coach Knight, one story that has not been told is ours, about the managers who worked behind the scenes countless hours at Assembly Hall and beyond, wanting to make our contribution to the success of Indiana Basketball. We had a unique vantage point. We were not recruited to fill a spot on the roster, but we literally had the seat directly behind Coach at home games hearing what the best mind in the game was saying, spent time in the basketball office, in the coaches locker room, escorted visiting teams and game officials, and spent considerable time on the road transporting dignitaries from the sports world to and from Bloomington. From our unique position, we saw and participated in many of the innovations Coach developed to find a new edge in competition, while always abiding by the rules of the game almost religiously faithful to its core values.

Throughout our experiences, enriched by all that proximity, we learned many lessons that we all call upon throughout our personal and professional lives as adults. We are productive citizens. Our graduation rate is as high as the players' (leading all of college basketball). Our contribution to our families and communities is considerable. This book has been written to share with Coach Knight, and others who may read it, how remarkable we found the education we absorbed behind those curtains and gates that surrounded the court at Assembly Hall. Coach Knight delegated a great deal of responsibility to his managerial staff, and held us to the same high performance standards he set for himself and the team.

This book is organized by the decades that Coach Knight was at Indiana. At the start of each decade is a feature essay written by a member of the IU Basketball community followed by individual essays written by the managers on Coach Knight's staff. Included in each section are memories and favorite moments we experienced, a few pictures also included put faces to the names in the book. The manager essays, short to long, were written with limited guidance to ensure each person told his story his way.

Throughout this book you will find certain phrases repeated and themes emerge as you read this history of Indiana Basketball. It is apparent, that from his first practice at Indiana to his last, Coach Knight set high expectations, and worked hard to achieve them. As our title suggests, "prepare to win" was a mantra for all of us in the basketball program because Coach taught us that while everyone wants to win, it is those who have the will to prepare to win that are victorious. And we were among the elite in preparation in college basketball.

The 1971–2000 Indiana Basketball managers want to collectively thank Coach Knight and Indiana University for our taste of true uniqueness as participants in and beneficiaries of the great sports tradition that is Indiana Basketball.

Dave Skibinski
Altadena, California

Foreword by Bob Knight

Our managers were extremely intelligent and hardworking kids during the time I coached. We were very fortunate to have such great managers. Their dedication toward the various demanding and time-consuming jobs, in addition to their classroom work, was actually an inspiration to our players to work as hard as the managers did. We had the same high expectations of our managers as we did of our players, which helped them learn valuable lessons after basketball for the game of life. They were able to translate those lessons into personal and professional success. Many of them went on to coaching at various levels from junior high school to the NBA.

I am equally proud of the success of our managers away from basketball. They have gone on to be successful in their adult lives as doctors, lawyers, educators, public servants, corporate executives and entrepreneurs.They became a part of our program because of their love of basketball and each manager, in his own way, made a tremendous contribution to the success of our teams. I always felt that our managerial staff was a very, very important part of what we did and I am extremely proud of all they have accomplished since graduating.

Bob Knight

Acknowledgements

Preparing a book of this sort is never a single person venture. This book is no exception. The first thank you goes to all the managers that had the time and desire to contribute to the book. There was a very high level of interest from the onset of the project that we should do this, and the routine encouragement to push forward was equally appreciated.

Second, we all owe years, in fact decades of gratitude to Coach Knight's administrative assistant, MaryAnn Davis. She has been a trusted friend, confidant, advocate, mentor, and so many other things to the managers over the years. Her good humor always got us through tense moments within the program, and her cool thinking and steady hand guided us when the waters were rough, especially inside the basketball office. MaryAnn was instrumental in our engagement with Coach Knight for this project. From all of us, we say thank you!

Third, when we decided to launch this project we needed a second set of eyes on all the initial drafts of content for the book. A special thank you goes out to Michael McGlothlin, Brian Miller, Nelson Nettles, Steve Skoronski and Daniel Zweig for agreeing to do the initial reading and editing of the essays that were submitted. They were the first filter to ensure the quality of the content for this endeavor. And thanks to those managers who submitted images for inclusion in this book.

Fourth, we also thank Bob Hammel, longtime sportswriter and friend to the legion of managers that worked for Coach Knight at Indiana. Bob has been a steadfast supporter of our efforts and could always be trusted for a correct reading of the pulse within Indiana Basketball. We all spent many hours in Assembly Hall and on the road with Bob and we thank you for being our comrade. When we contacted Bob about not only contributing to the book but also editing the full manuscript, he enthusiastically responded with yes in less than 24 hours. Bob, thank you for your professional skills in helping refine the writings of all the "amateur writers" who primarily contributed to this effort.

Fifth, we would like to thank the Athletic Department at Indiana University, especially one from our ranks, Assistant Athletic Director Scott Dolson. When we approached Scott about the project, he was instrumental as our liaison to get the records we needed to get in touch with the manager corps. Scott, we say thanks to you and everyone at IU that helped.

Sixth, we thank Glen Grunwald for also contributing a feature essay for the book. Glen was always a friend to the managerial corps and his quiet, intelligent and good humor was always a dose of tonic at just the right moment. Glen was generous to us during his playing days and has been a friend and resource to many since our graduation. Tim Garl was the supervisor of the managers, along with the recently deceased former trainer Bob Young. The head trainer at IU wears many hats while working for Coach Knight, and both Bob and Tim treated us with respect and often kept us out of harms way, or pulled us from its grip when things went awry. When we reached out to Tim to write a feature for the book, he too enthusiastically agreed to help. Thank you, Tim and Glen, for making valuable contributions to this book.

Seventh, we would like to thank all the support staff with whom we worked over the years at IU, including the sports information staff, business office, ticket office and facilities department. We especially thank Red Grow and Warren McGuire, the long-time equipment managers with whom we spent many hours and were friendly and jovial, and enjoyed giving us a hard time about getting things done on time. We must also thank all the assistant basketball coaches with whom we worked and with whom many of us interviewed to earn our spot on the managerial roster. We also thank you for your professional courtesies as many of you that left IU for your own head coaching positions took many of us with you as members of your own staff. We thank you for your confidence then and for your continued friendship today.

Rather than name some good friends and miss many others that worked throughout Assembly Hall, let us just say thank you to all the athletic department staff that guided and supported our efforts throughout the Bob Knight era. Believe us when we say we couldn't have done our jobs without you.

Lastly, we thank Coach Knight for joining us in this effort. We trust that our collective success is just one of the many markers that chronicle his career. As you will read from this book, we are undoubtedly among Coach Knight's most enthusiastic supporters and we value greatly all the lessons we learned being part of Indiana Basketball. Coach, thank you for the opportunity of a lifetime.

Indiana Basketball Manager Roster
from 1971-2003

    We have endeavored to include the names of all the managers that worked for Coach Knight over his years at Indiana. To those that were omitted it is simply an oversight as we did not have rosters to consult from our "playing days."

1972	Than H. Lenox
1973	George G. Graessle, III
1974	Jack J. Gabor
1974	John L. Liston
1974	Ed Paternoster
1975	Larry G. Sherfick
1975	Todd E. Woodruff
1975	Lawrence G. Cannon
1976	Brad M. Winters
1976	Chuck Swenson
1976	Tim Walker
1976	Mark A. Siegal
1977	Kim C. Kohlmeier
1977	Russell Bright
1978	Brian D. Miller
1978	Gerry Freitas
1978	Daniel J. Zweig
1978	Rex C. Taylor
1979	Brad Cummins

1979	Andy Dean
1979	Marc Goodman
1979	Dave Macer
1979	Jim Stanbrough
1980	Chris J. Stone
1980	John P. Levenda
1980	Peter G. Schroeder
1980	David J. Skibinski
1981	David Armstrong
1981	Stephen M. Skoronski
1982	Joe Black
1982	Gary D. Sims
1982	David Skirvin
1983	Michael S. Agee
1983	Charles E. Fattore
1983	Mark D. Galenski
1984	Jerome E. Davis, Jr.
1984	Michael A. Fox
1984	Joseph Gleissner
1984	Jon Jennings
1985	Jeffrey A. Buckley
1985	Christopher E. Kaiser
1985	Gregory A. Ryan
1986	Joe Csenar
1986	James D. Kelly
1986	Scott Perlson
1986	Jeffrey D. Stuckey
1987	Mike Adkins
1987	Craig Hartman
1987	John W. Himebrook

1987	Michael J. McGlothlin
1987	Mark Sims
1988	Scott M. Dolson
1988	David J. Gottlieb
1989	Nelson A. Nettles
1989	Stephen C. Trust
1989	John E. Martin
1989	Gregory E. Burton
1990	Michael J. Hall
1990	L.J. Wright
1990	Michael B. Kelly
1991	John D. Cowan
1992	Joseph M. Areddy, Jr.
1992	Troy A. Boshears
1992	Lawrence A. Frank
1992	Mark Johnson
1992	Chris O'Hagan
1992	Jonathan C. Stuckey
1992	Brent A. Thompson
1993	Curtis R. Simic, Jr.
1993	Martin A. Pollio
1993	Matthew Greene
1993	Joseph N. Abunassar
1994	Walton Muyumba
1994	Jason F. Davis
1994	Matthew T. Bowen
1995	Brian T. Zapach
1996	Ryan Carr
1996	George David
1996	Brian Hahn

1996	Kevin J. Lemme
1996	Shane Garman
1996	Shea M. Rink
1997	Dave Owens
1997	Muuka M. Muyumba
1998	Robert J. Housel
1998	Ryan F. Michaelis
1998	VaShone Rhodes
1998	Michael P. Schrage
1998	Joshua K. Shanklin
1999	Rob L. Bakalar
1999	Joe Pasternack
1999	Jeremiah J. Shirk
2000	Matt Babrick
2000	Kyle Bailey
2000	Dusty A. May
2000	Andy Murphy
2001	Daniel J. Block, Jr.
2001	Chris Giffin
2001	Theodore Hodges, IV
2001	Jason Imes
2001	Thomas Labadie
2001	David Pillar
2002	Jason Buckner
2002	Brandon Sorrell
2003	Josh Emily

Classes of
1971-1979

Bob Hammel

Bob Hammel is a legend among sports journalists, and the eyes and ears of Indiana University Sports fans for three decades. He was the Sports Editor and Columnist of the *Bloomington Herald-Times* from 1966-1996. Prior to covering the Hoosiers, he was with newspapers in Huntington, Fort Wayne, Kokomo and Indianapolis. In May of 1995, he received the highest honor given to a basketball writer, the Curt Gowdy Award, from the Naismith Hall of Fame in Springfield, Mass. Has been selected the top sportswriter in Indiana 15 times by the National Sportswriters and Sportscasters Association. He is a member of the Indiana Basketball Hall of Fame and the Indiana Journalism Hall of Fame. He has written eight books about Hoosier basketball, including *Beyond the Brink with Indiana* (IUP, 1987) and *A Banner Year* (IUP, 1993); he was also the editor of the *Bob Hammel Indiana Basketball Magazine*. With Bob Knight, he co-authored *Knight: My Story, and The Power of Negative Thinking*.

The Worker Bees with Notepads ... and Memories

There's a good chance you didn't know that the all-time record for consecutive wins at the start of an NBA coach's career is 13, and it's held by a man whose preparation to be a coach came under Bob Knight at Indiana University.

Not as a player under Bob Knight. Lawrence Frank, who coached the New Jersey Nets to that winning streak—at the time a record for a beginning coach or manager in any American major league sport—was a four-year manager in Knight's Indiana program.

Knight's managers, in his 29-year tenure at Indiana that raised basketball excellence and success to a level unmatched in Big Ten history, comprised a fraternity unlike any other on campus, but no less bonded than anything Greek. There were from 12 to 18 for every team, moving like the players up a stairway of responsibility and expectations during their coinciding academic passage through IU. Senior Manager was the pinnacle, of authority and of responsibility.

What that experience led to in life achievements is the remarkable consistency of this voluntary "we-should-write-a-book" project. The roles they played were similar, so many of their stories are. But very many of them, too, break off into adventures that left lasting (1) impressions, (2) scars, (3) learning experiences, or a combination of same, or something quite special and unique to a certain few, and to all.

They are memories, and this is a book of them. I read and I picture an IU practice, any of the hundreds I saw over those years: Bob Knight's classroom, where there are no distractions, where the player concentration is intense, and where a dozen or up young men of varied athletic backgrounds themselves play their own vital roles on-court and off, as inconspicuously— oh, believe me, hopefully, prayerfully inconspicuously—but as efficiently as possible. You'll read of one's adventure wearing a puka shell necklace at a game—once, never again. And another's clear memory of time spent in the 2 a.m. area in a frigid and dark airport with the team, and The Coach, waiting on a mis-sent bus. And the quick thinking in a dark and vacant coach's office at Ohio State that averted an eight-hour waste. And the one among them who actually suited up and played in 16 games, even scored on a back-door cut that brought a clap—a singular but unbelievably pleasing clap—from The Coach. And ... oh, just read.

Read these gems from men who now are doctors and lawyers and CEOs, and—in highly impressive numbers—NBA or college or high school coaches, benefiting still from those notepads they kept in their pockets while working practices, taking down notes when they could on the singularly effective coaching techniques and tactical thoughts of, in the eyes of many, the best teacher they had on campus.

Brothers all, these Special Fraternity members. Are there Latin symbols for Tutored, Proud and Grateful? With a sprinkle of wit that factors in the fun element of an education like none other.

Bob Hammel, Basketball Writer
Bloomington Herald-Times

Than Lenox

President, T.H. Lenox
Lebanon, Indiana
IU Manager: 1967-72
Degree Earned: B.S., Zoology, Indiana University, 1972

Than Lenox has enjoyed a career in business since his graduation from Indiana University. Early in his career he was involved in the family owned Lenox Lincoln-Mercury for over 20 years. He has also been an active real estate investor providing affordable living to local residents specializing in condominiums and rentals.

Think About It

What always impressed me about Coach Knight is how he would get down to basic components of a situation (defense) and make so much sense out of it and make it work. About two weeks into preseason practice in Coach Knight's first year—one of the players (won't name names—but he had the highest GPA) asked why Coach emphasized defense. Coach screams back—"Think about it, Frank!!!!" (So much for names) Well, Frank thought about it for a while and could not come up with anything, but hell—with Coach around—it was a little hard to think sometimes. Then Coach elaborates—"Think about it, Frank!!! If you hold your opponent to zero what is the worst that can happen." Frank couldn't come up with that answer either; I think he was a little intimidated. (Really) "Frank, if you hold your opponent to zero, the worst you can do is tie. When you hold your opponent to zero you can never lose. My ultimate goal is to shut someone out."

"Think about it, Frank!!!"

Well of course! You could score a bunch of points, but your opponent could score one more and you lose. But if you hold your opponent to zero, and you score one point you will always win. And you can't lose.

Of course, thinking you could shut someone out just seemed ridiculous.

However, the 1971-72 Notre Dame team came in as the opponent in the Dedication game for Assembly Hall with first-year Coach Digger Phelps. Notre Dame, the year before as I recall, had Austin Carr and some other good players and went deep in the NCAA Tournament. However all those players were gone, and Digger said to me as he left the shoot around Friday evening, "We are just going to get killed."

The next afternoon, he was right. Notre Dame actually led 5-4, then it was 28-7, and 51-13 and it kept going. We reversed the score on them, and added a bucket. The final score: Indiana 94-Notre Dame 29. John Ritter out-scored Notre Dame 32-29. That night made me a believer that defense will always win—and Coach Knight made it work. From that point on I would always try to analyze any situation from more than one point of view; from all angles.

George Graessle, III

President & CEO, Graessle-Mercer Company
Seymour, Indiana
IU Manager: 1969-1973
Degree Earned: B.S., Management, Indiana University, 1973

George Graessle entered the golf industry working as an assistant for one year following graduation from Indiana University. In the fall of 1974 he entered the business world with Graessle-Mercer and where he today holds the position of President and CEO. He holds the distinction of serving under Coach Lou Watson for two years and also worked under Coach Bob Knight in his first two seasons at Indiana.

Always Prepared

The best experience being around Coach Knight was seeing how well he prepared for every day. Each day at practice, he had a sheet, written in a red felt pen, that had the day's schedule for practice on it and he followed it for the most part to the minute. I still have some of those sheets to this day.

Before any game IU played, it was great to watch him prepare each player and to prepare the team for that particular opponent, with different approaches as we headed into each game. He prepared not only for what IU did the best, but also for what the other team did best and then tried to take that away from the other team.

In a business like I am in, scheduling is a huge part of every day and every hour and problems that can come up during busy periods must all be taken care of ahead of time. Coach Knight was always prepared for just about anything and anyone. Preparation has always helped me with everything in my life and this came from being around Coach Knight and the IU program.

As part of preparation for a game on the road, we always practiced the day before on the opposing team's court. We were to play Kentucky, at Louisville, not Lexington, and were at Freedom Hall getting ready for practice. Kentucky had finished practice about an hour before that but many people were still there when IU took the court.

We had only nine players for that practice so coach looked at me and said "suit up." I thought my moment had arrived. I realized we brought no extra practice uniforms, just an extra game uniform so that is what I put on, along with a pair of Steve Downing's extra shoes. The team was still shooting when I took the court, needless to say, to the laughter of many. I could hear some of the Kentucky fans wondering who I was. I tried to get a couple of shots in but Coach Bliss laughed and said not to worry, I wasn't going to get any shots. My only job was to guard John Ritter. Unfortunately, he ran the baseline the whole time and I was running out of breath. However, I did knock the ball out of Downing's hands twice. Coach Knight stopped practice and said, "Steve, if Graessle can knock the ball out of your hands, what do you think Kentucky will do?" Steve didn't like this too well and set a couple of screens on me I still remember today. Steve Downing went on to have his best college game ever—47 points and 25 rebounds playing every second as IU won the game 90-89, in two overtime periods.

Jack Gabor, M.S.

Team Camp Director, Valparaiso University
Valparaiso, IN
IU Manager: 1971-1974
IU Graduate Assistant Coach: 1977-78
Degrees Earned: B.S., HPER, Indiana University, 1974
M.S., Secondary Education, Indiana University
Northwest, 1981

Jack Gabor has been a high school educator and coach for over 30 years in the state of Indiana. He has been the Head boys basketball coach at Bishop Noll, Huntington North, Kankakee Valley, and Griffith high schools. In 23 years as a head basketball coach Gabor's teams were 334-177 winning 7 sectional titles and 3 conference championships. Gabor was also head baseball coach at Bishop Noll with a combined record of 283-99, winning 7 sectionals, 2 regionals, and 10 conference championships. His total won – lost record as a varsity coach is 617-286 (68.3%). Gabor is one of only 2 people to take a boys basketball team and baseball team to the Final Four. He has also coached the Indiana All-Star team in both basketball and baseball. Gabor has been named a COY 8 times in his career. He is now retired and serves as Team Camp Director for the Valparaiso University Men's basketball program.

The Man and His Method. So Misunderstood!

My gosh, where do I begin? Besides my parents, there has never been an individual other than Coach Knight who has helped create and shape my beliefs towards success. Due to the privacy that Coach has always maintained, a lot of people will never know the funny and compassionate side of Coach. They only know of the challenging (but funny now) ways he got the most out of his people. There was never a simple way to get out of things gone bad—in fact, you can't imagine the number of times the words "what are we gonna do now?" were muttered. I will offer a few examples of this motivation.

One of my seasons as a manager, Coach had me doing a lot of office work, film exchanges and helping out with his two sons, Tim and Patrick. One day I picked them up from school to bring them to practice. Practice days were never dull, as one of Coach's friends like a Pete Newell or some friends from

Ohio would just happen to be there. Naturally everyone wanted to be at their best. Now we all knew what a great fan of the Celtics he was, because of his friendship with John Havlicek. On this particular day all was going well and I arrived with Tim and Patrick at practice. I parked Coach's car in his normal spot in front of Assembly Hall, and got to practice like I had a million times before. I gave Coach his keys and started to walk away when all of a sudden this loud voice lashed out at me with a shrill—"JACK"—stopping me in my footsteps. Practice was still going on, but it didn't seem to matter as his only concern was "where the hell is the Celtic insignia?" (on his keychain that Havlicek had given him). I was promptly informed that I needed to find it or? Needless to say this was one of those moments. I searched all over the car, and even Tim and Patrick helped. We also enlisted the help of his secretary, MaryAnn Davis, but to no avail. Finally, someone had the idea to call Coach's wife, Nancy. After a brief conversation she told us that it had been falling off the past week, and asked if that's what we were looking for? She had found it on the ground in the morning after he had left for work. So I hurried to his house to get it, I returned to practice to proudly tell Coach (and be the hero who saved the day—Not!); the only response I got was a mild "OK." Believe me that *was* OK, as I survived the challenge put forth to me and all was good again in B-town.

During my Graduate Assistant year I had another of those moments. Whenever we went on the road we needed receipts to cover everything. I was assigned to take one of our coaches, Joby Wright, to Gary, Indiana to look at a possible recruit. On the way back, I put off doing the smart thing—refueling—and, during those days of gas shortages, stations rarely stayed open late. We had already slid off the road due to the weather and had been towed. As you may have surmised, I ran out of gas, had to walk to an open station, get a ride back to the car and finish refueling. The next day I was obviously worried about the amount of the expense I was going to turn in and asked MaryAnn if she might sugar coat things for me with Coach a bit (it was pricey). She said she would try and all I could do was hope for a good day. She was the best, and if anyone could help you in a jam with Coach she was the one. So I came to the office after class, trying to make a quiet entrance, but Coach was waiting. As I walked in I heard the infamous "JACK!" Coach was reading something with his back to me, my expense report, of course, and in his typical sarcastic way asked me how in the hell this trip had cost so much? I thought to myself to just man-up, no stupid excuses, and tried to explain, fully. After a short time (which seemed to last forever), his lone response was a soft "OK, just wondering." Once again I had been challenged and tested, and I had won; I handled the pressure. Of course after I left the office every coach wanted to know what happened, a little look on their face saying, "Now wasn't that fun?" They knew they had me. Thank God I had gone to church on Sunday.

During the '73-'74 season, highly recruited Indiana High School Mr. Basketball Kent Benson was in his freshman year. After our success in the previous year's Final Four, expectations were running wild for the upcoming season. However, we were not playing that great by Christmas as the year before after losing in the Far West Classic and now having to open the Big Ten season at Michigan. We went up to Ann Arbor, and blew a fifteen point half-time lead in the Big Ten opener and lost, 73-71, and Benson never got in the game. No doubt the trip back would be a long, quiet one. In this case the longer the better. There would be a lot of soul-searching, and a whole lot of practice. When we arrived back at Assembly Hall, we gathered in the locker room as usual. After listening to Coach describe our poor level of play, we were told that we would have multiple practices the next day starting at 6 a.m. (a rarity). He said we would stay until we got it right. The first practice didn't go well and was short-lived. At a later practice, Coach was wondering out loud how a 6' 10" Mr. Basketball was unable to get to the free-throw line in his first 14 college games. How he needed to realize that he was playing for an NCAA championship and not against a bunch of big Indiana farm boys. I think this is when his famous quote "when ass meets bench, the brain starts to think" became famous. The team rallied around Benny, and would go on to win their next 12 games, with Benny being voted the MVP. We finished 23-5 that year and Co-Champs of the Big Ten, then won the Conference Commissioner's Association Tournament. What a great example of his motivational ways.

This whole scenario was bad enough, but sometime during this period one of the most incredible things occurred. You all know about Coach Knight's history as a high school punter. Coach was holding a basketball when a turnover occurred. Enraged, he punted the basketball high into the air in Assembly Hall. All eyes were on the ball as it was bouncing back down the seats ever-so-neatly into a wastebasket near mid-court. Now considering all that has gone on, I can assure you that we did everything we could to stop from busting out laughing, and fortunately we were able to hold it in. Finally, those magic words "locker room" were heard. I really think that our team's speed increased at that moment. Fortunately, the coaches went off to another direction and I was told to go to tell the team when the next practice would be. When I got to the locker room, I was met with a sigh of relief that it was me and not Coach Knight, as they were all rolling in laughter and amazement. It was one of the most astonishing sights I had ever seen on a basketball court. The next practice was quite a bit better!

Preparation

What Coach has taught me over the course of nearly 40 years in this profession was that the road to success isn't as complicated as many make it out to be. You all are familiar with his saying that "The key is not the will to win ... everybody has that. It is the will to prepare to win that is important." One of the first things I picked up on was the amount of preparation that goes into not just each game but each and every practice. As we all know the world is competitive, and the willingness to pay close attention to detail in your preparation will usually provide you with success. However, you can't do it alone, and teamwork is the key to accomplishing that. The hours put in by coaches and players alike will always remain thankless. Fans only see the final result, and think that was easy! The tireless hours of film watching, meetings and practice planning that goes on aren't known. People would be amazed at how many times match-ups could change during the week prior to the game. In order for their preparation to work, there must be teamwork, and if people are going to work together on the same page. They must be loyal to one another.

Loyalty

This may be the most memorable moment for me, and certainly the best example I provide to people who don't know the other side of Coach, and about why I am so loyal to him. We had finished practicing for the Mid-East Regional ('72-'73) and were walking off the court to board the bus to the airport. It was spring break on campus so not much else going on. Coach was walking across the court at Assembly Hall, when he asked me what I was going to do now. I had voluntarily stayed for practice and had the option to go home or just stay on campus. Coach asked me if I wanted to go to the game, and my response was "Yes, but I don't have a ticket or transportation." He reached into his pocket, flipped me his keys, and said, "Get my car to Nashville and we'll take it from there." Credit cards are in the glove compartment, which I knew from experience. What a rush was going through me at this point, I was going to the NCAA Tourney! Coach could have easily rented a car there, but was showing me how to reward people who are loyal to you without making a big fuss. I can guarantee no one knows this story, because Coach wasn't doing this to get attention, and hardly anyone seeks out the good things he has done for people. I thought, "Wow, could it get any better than this?" The answer, YES.

Once I got to Nashville, I handed over the keys. From that point on I went with the team everywhere, and we would go on to beat Marquette and Kentucky for the Mid-East Regional Championship. There would not be a long drive home as Coach liked to get away from the team after a big win and go hunting or fishing. As we were getting ready to leave for home, Coach asked me for the keys and told me to fly home with the team, and make sure I was ready for St. Louis next week. We were going to the Final Four! That same scenario was duplicated the next week, and would be my first encounter with a Final Four at any level. The icing on the cake to all of this as the season wound down, was when MaryAnn called me into the office and said she needed to get my ring size. Outside of my wedding ring, this is my most prized possession: a 1972-1973 Big Ten and NCAA Mid-East Regional Championship ring.

What it symbolized to me was not a few wins, but how to treat people.

I have taken this life-lesson and tried to live up to it in my own career, helping my former players and students as much as I could, and looking for that quality in people when putting together a staff. It is much easier to be yourself when you know you are surrounded by loyalty. I will never forget this lesson, and it is part of the reason you can be yourself if you have people behind you. Even though I have never needed it, it gave me the courage to do what I thought was right without the fear of any repercussions. The importance of that is something I feel is often overlooked when analyzing a person's success.

Do You Want To Be Liked Or Respected?

I remember Coach calling me into his office a few days before I was to leave campus to do my student teaching and asking me what my plans were. All of a sudden out of the blue he asked me "Jack, is it more important for you to be liked or respected?" My response was to be respected. He said, "Good, because if it were the former, then you are entering the wrong profession." That was some of the best advice he could have given me. His simple reasoning was that you are gonna cut more kids then keep, so a coach's popularity level never looks too promising right from the start, and (unless you are a legend), it doesn't get any better. Over my career, I have seen this play out time and again with some really good coaches with great records victimized by someone else's agenda. You must be your own man, able to stand for what you believe and not some administrative puppet whose use will always run out. That's why I said earlier, knowing they have a guy like Coach behind them allows people from his program to be themselves and do what they feel is the right thing to do no matter what profession they choose. A person working from a position of confidence will always be a strong leader, give direction, and make tough decisions, something we coaches do daily.

Teacher, Disciplinarian, Competitor

Finally, once you get out on the floor and try to find yourself, Coach Knight always felt that if a coach could do these three things he would be on his way to having a great career. One of the most important things he taught me about coaching was that a good coach is always a good teacher. Kids learn in different ways today and often need different types of explanations. I remember him saying that there will be seasons when as a coach you have to spend much more time teaching than coaching your team, especially when you are dealing with a really young team. He instilled in me that it was more important to teach what I know, rather than knowing a lot but not getting it across to my team. Over my career studying other coaches, this seems to be very true not just in the won-lost records, but in the futures of the student-athletes whose lives you have touched and what they have become. Some of my best teams started off this very way and I think education would be better off today if we followed this philosophy. Teach well what you know.

Over the years, Coach was known as a strong disciplinarian. Some people didn't quite understand the true meaning of that, thus he was most often characterized as this harsh, ruthless coach. Truth be told, his true meaning of the word discipline was simply to do the right thing when needed, every time. He believed being fundamentally sound on the court was a form of discipline. It didn't matter if it was staying low in a stance, blocking-out, making the correct pass and reading a cut that was available, or shot selection. All these fundamentals took discipline to execute at the right time and place, and failure to do so was lacking the discipline needed to be successful. All of the time he put into drilling his teams fundamentally and the organization of practices and films, to scouting reports were all examples of what his meaning of discipline was and not the laps, suspensions, and in your face methods that most media wanted America to know and relate to him.

Finally, as I have given some earlier examples, Coach was always challenging your competitiveness. It didn't matter if it was a game of HORSE or vying for the Big Ten Title. Whether it was looking for a key chain or an explanation, he was always challenging you to be the best you could be at all times. He never wanted you to be satisfied, and pushed you to reach your potential, whatever that might be. One thing is for sure, is that if you were part of the program, you would come as close to reaching your potential as possible.

Thank You Coach

I cannot say enough about the impact that Coach has had on my life, and sincerely thank him for the opportunities that have come my way. He not only taught me the game of basketball, but how to succeed at the game of life. Without the opportunities he provided, my life would be totally different. The training ground for me back then gave me the firsthand experiences that no book, video, or professor could provide.

I have never met a person who can break things down so clearly and concisely. Often times I would think to myself "Hey, why didn't I think of that?" I often ask myself, "What would Coach think about this?" To some, his methods may be unique; I merely view them as the norm. The items I mentioned only scratch the surface of all the things he taught me.

I always chuckle these days now that Coach is part of the Media, and acquaintances (previously not big fans) will say, "Hey he's pretty good." They are finally getting to know the other side of Coach, whom I regard as one of the smartest men in the world. My response is, "Well if you think that was good, how would you like to have lived it for 4 years?" I LOVED IT! Thanks, Coach, for always being there and helping me become who I am today!

John Liston

Retired Educator, Downers Grove North High School
Downers Grove, IL
IU Manager: 1970-74
Degree Earned: B.S., Health and Safety, Indiana University, 1974

John Liston is a retired high school teacher who resides in Downers Grove, Illinois. John was an IU Basketball manager from 1970 till 1974. He and Jack Gabor served as co-head managers during the 1973-74 IU Basketball season. After graduating from IU with a B.S. in Health and Safety Education in 1974, John worked for Community High School District #99 at Downers Grove North High School for thirty-three years. During his teaching career, John was the first athletic trainer at Downers Grove North and also taught health and driver education. John is married to Sandy Hanna Liston (IU Class of 1976) and has a son, Sean Liston (IU Class of 2011).

From the Start

One of my favorite basketball memories was being in Assembly Hall for the first basketball game to be played in the venue. I enjoyed the noise of the crowd in the seats, the lights reflecting on the floor, the IU players in their striped warm-up pants, "mopping" the floor at halftime, and the excitement of being part of the Indiana University Basketball tradition on that day in 1971. This memory somehow dimmed over the years, then your son calls one evening and wants to tell you something he saw on ESPN. "Dad, I was watching a video clip on ESPN about Quinn Buckner and I saw you! I Saw YOU! You were on the bench with Coach Knight, Bob Young...and the players." Yeah, memories suddenly become crystal clear. IU Basketball, Coach Knight, and Assembly Hall still hold a lot of good memories for me and my family.

During the summer of 1973, I was taking a couple of summer school classes when I unexpectedly was asked to go with the IU Basketball team and Coach Knight to Spain and the Canary Islands to play some exhibition games. Quinn Buckner was going to China. I suppose I was asked to go to Spain because I lived close to Bloomington and I was also a student trainer working under the team trainer Bob Young. I dropped my classes and was off with the team.

Essays

After driving one of the assistant basketball coach's cars to Chicago to process passports for myself and some of the team members, and then following a few days of practice, we were flown to New York's LaGuardia Airport on the IU plane. After an afternoon boat tour around New York City, we were taken to Kennedy Airport and a TWA 747 whisked us to Madrid that evening. In Madrid, the memories were many … a couple of basketball games with club teams … sightseeing in Madrid and Toledo … washing uniforms in the hotel … a bus trip and games on the Costa De Sol. We played a game in one arena and they didn't have towels for showers. So a janitor went home, got some towels and brought them back to us to use after the game. It was definitely the "ultimate" road trip for me, being in a foreign country for the first time, and practicing and playing teams in a different town every day or so, and living out of a suitcase.

The team traveled on to the Canary Islands and played a couple of games and we saw the sights. On our departure from the Canaries our flight was delayed because of fog, and we missed our TWA flight back to New York and thus our connecting flight to Indianapolis. In order to make alternate arrangements, we had to make an overseas call to the IU Basketball office and stayed overnight in Madrid at an airport hotel. We flew out the next day to New York, cleared customs and immigration and flew on to Indianapolis.

It was one of those "once in a lifetime" trips with the IU Basketball team and I was honored and privileged to have been asked to go. Thanks, Quinn, for going to China. And yes, I still had to take summer school classes the next year to complete my degree on time.

All our team meals were usually pre-arranged with the hotel where we were staying for away games. During a "road trip" to Ohio State in the 1973-74 basketball season, Coach Knight decided to have the team eat at a different restaurant in Columbus. So we called the hotel to tell them we wouldn't be eating at their restaurant, and made reservations for the team to order off the menu at the restaurant Coach Knight suggested. Coach Knight and the other coaches proceeded to go and scout high school players that evening. We all arrived at the "new" restaurant and after being seated, I found the manager and asked if he would bill the IU athletic department, and I would sign the receipt when we were leaving. The manager (definitely

17

an Ohio State Buckeye fan) said "no" we couldn't bill the meals and that the tab had to be paid in full upon our departure. I didn't have enough "travel cash" from the university to cover a non-prearranged meal, but I did have an "emergency" personal family American Express card that my father had given me. So, I charged the meals to my father's card. I think my father kept that American Express bill and the check receipt from the IU athletic department for a few months as a memento.

Larry Sherfick, M.S.

School Counselor, Shoals Community School Corporation
Shoals, Indiana
IU Manager: 1971-1975
Degrees Earned: B.S., Education, Indiana University, 1975
M.S., Education, Indiana University, 1980
Specialist, School Counseling, Indiana University 1990

Larry Sherfick has worked for the Shoals Community School Corporation for 36 years. He is currently the school counselor for the junior and senior high school.

Witnessing the Birth of Hoosier Nation

My freshman year at Indiana University began in August 1971. A few months earlier IU had hired a new basketball coach out of West Point, New York, named Bob Knight.

As I look back on it now, I went into becoming a basketball manager as a way of extending my love affair with the game beyond high school. My manager application consisted of writing a letter to the basketball office inquiring about the opportunity. I received a reply directing me to contact Than Lenox, who would be the senior manager for the 1971-72 season. That was the extent of the process that led me to a position that would impact me for the rest of my life.

As soon as I arrived on campus, I made contact with Than and began meeting other managers. It was all new to me, including Assembly Hall, which was still undergoing the finishing touches before the building's grand opening. That year practice began in the "new" field house, where IU had played the previous ten seasons. The older managers delighted in having us newbies constantly sweep the floor to keep the dust down. It was a welcome relief to move into Assembly Hall and practice there. An early highlight of the first year was IU's victory over Kentucky at Freedom Hall.

During practice, managers served at the will of the coaching staff, helping out in drills and especially in getting a deflected ball back into the hands of a player or coach as quickly as possible. I began learning from Day 1 how important organization and planning was in developing a competitive team. Managers were usually the first people on the floor, bringing out the balls and sweeping the court. I would often help the equipment managers, Red Grow and Warren McGwire, with practice gear. Managers were usually the ones who tried to explain away the missing socks that seemed to disappear throughout the year. It was a routine managers settled into and mostly enjoyed, unless the team was having a bad practice. Coach took no prisoners when concentration was lacking, be it with a player not paying attention or a couple of managers loafing on the sidelines. We were all expected to give 100 percent.

Coach Knight would tell us that mental is to physical as 4 is to 1, when emphasizing the importance of mental preparation compared to physical talent. I have taken this as gospel in my own life and tried to pass it along as sound advice.

The years went by quickly, with Coach Knight accomplishing the goals he and his staff were setting for the players they had recruited. It was fascinating to see Coach's vision of basketball evolve. Watching how man-to-man defense was taught, broken down individually, and augmented with rules and responsibilities involving all players helping and recovering. It was an excellent example of teaching at the highest level. Witnessing the birth of the motion offense and again seeing how the concept was taught through drills using whole, part, whole methods of instruction, was an ideal environment to learn the game and witness excellent teaching. Coach Knight was the best professor I ever studied under while at IU. When I watch a basketball game now and hear reference to "running the motion offense" it makes me proud to know I was there when it was brand new.

Being Senior Manager for the 1974-1975 team remains one of the highlights of my life. There is seldom a day that goes by that I do not reflect on something that happened during that wonderful season. I suppose I can safely say that the amount of responsibility I had to assume made a man out of me, at least the man I have become. Because of my association with Coach Knight and the opportunities I had managing the team, I developed the confidence and experience to teach and become an effective leader. Highlights of the '74-'75 season included a trip to Hawaii to play in the Rainbow Classic. What a thrill! Going undefeated until the 92-90 loss to Kentucky in the NCAA Regional Final was a sad end to a tremendous season of basketball. Coach Knight has often said he counts the 1975 Hoosiers among the best college teams ever assembled.

After college I returned to the community where I grew up in southern Indiana and to our family farm. During quail hunting season, Coach Knight would count on me to "have the birds ready and in shape" for his trips afield. It was a joy for my farmer father and our neighbors to have Coach Knight as their guest. I recall a cold, snowy Sunday afternoon in January when coach and his hunting companion, Jack Brannon, came by. Jack decided to wait in the truck, while Coach hunted with their dogs, walking purposely along the fence rows through the wildlife plots set aside especially for Coach. He returned to the truck, empty handed, but insisted it was the most fun he had had hunting in quite a while. Coach was never one to shirk from a challenge, weather or otherwise. Though Coach no longer frequents our farm during hunting season, I still hear the quail call his name: Bob Knight!

Todd Woodruff, M.D.

Physician, Akron, Ohio

IU Manager: 1971-1975

Degrees Earned: B.A. Biology, Indiana University, 1975, M.D. Indiana University School of Medicine, 1979, Internship and Residency in Ophthalmology, Akron City Hospital, Akron, OH, 1983, Fellowship in Glaucoma, Columbia University, New York, NY, 1984

Todd Woodruff has spent 27 years in private practice as a physician and glaucoma specialist in Akron, OH; he retired from private practice in 2011. His medical career has been a mixture of private clinical practice, combined with medical education (instructor in glaucoma in the Summa Hospital ophthalmology residency program) and clinical research. Todd remains active in the medical field as Associate Professor of Ophthalmology, Northeast Ohio College of Medicine, a position he has held since 1984. He also currently serves as Interim Chairman of the Department of Ophthalmology, Summa Health System, Akron, Ohio (2011-present). Todd and his wife Adrianne have 2 children and 6 grandchildren.

Enter the Hurricane

We didn't have a warning ... not really. There were some articles that had been written about the new coach at Indiana. He was defense oriented and his Army teams had a reputation for toughness, but none of the managers, or the players for that matter, were prepared for the hurricane that was about to hit Indiana Basketball.

It was 1971 and Indiana was hoping for a new start after a disappointing 1970-71 season. At the end of that season, George McGinnis, the Indiana star sophomore, had turned pro, and Indiana brought in a young new coach, Bob Knight. With the loss of McGinnis, expectations for the new season were not high.

I had been brought up in the Indiana high school basketball culture, and tales of toughness regarding the new coach were not of any concern; toughness was an integral part of that culture. My brother had played high school basketball and had been a basketball manager from 1967 to 1971. He told me who to contact regarding getting a spot as manager. Unlike later years, after Coach Knight and the program gained national prominence, it was easy to get a managing spot, especially since my brother had worked with the new head manager, Than Lenox.

A friend and I from high school with whom I played basketball both got spots on the manager squad. We arranged our academic schedule so we would be free on most, if not all, afternoons and attend practice. The initial sacrifice of this schedule was that all our main courses had to be fit in the mornings, which meant we had to take early morning courses while our dorm-mates slept in.

From the start of school, before official practice began in October, we helped oversee physical training of the team. We never saw the coaches, and there was the usual easy going banter and joking among the players and managers that is the staple of sports. As could probably be said of most sports teams in high school and college in those days, it was a great group of guys, fun to be around.

The 1971-72 season was the last year that there were freshman basketball teams, and we freshman managers worked with the freshman team first, and then moved to the varsity practice later in the afternoon. Since the freshman team did not have 10 players, we managers who played basketball in high school got to fill out the slots during scrimmage. In this manner, we got to play against, and with, Steve Green (Green-o), John Laskowski (Laz), Steve Ahlfeld (Awful), and the others. Of course, they could eat us alive, but we got to be on the floor with them. The varsity was a different matter. The varsity was REALLY a different matter, for that was the domain of Robert M. Knight.

No one was prepared for the intensity, the intimidation, and the determination of Coach Knight. As a physician for the last 30 years I have worked in an occupation renowned for type-A personalities, but I have never met anyone as driven and focused as Coach Knight ... not even close! In a Coach Knight practice, there was no banter, no joking, not even any *talking* that was not focused on the job at hand. For week after week it was drills and more drills. Every move on the floor, on both offense and defense, had rules. Where you stand, how you defend your man when the basketball is on your side of the court, on the opposite side, how you change position as the ball moves, when you switch and when you don't. Some of this was familiar to anyone who played basketball in high school, but nothing this precise (and God protect anyone who did not follow the rules *precisely*).

Week after week these rules were pounded into the players through drills. There were no scrimmages. As the first game approached, the players grumbled that they hadn't actually *"played"* any basketball for weeks! Even when they worked on half-court offense or defense, seldom did more than 15 or 20 seconds pass without an outburst: "STOP! STOP!!! PEMBERTON! (or whoever) WHERE IS THE BALL?! WHERE IS THE F___ING BALL?!! WHERE ARE YOU SUPPOSED TO BE?!! HOW THE HELL MANY TIMES DO I HAVE TO TELL YOU GUYS?! GET YOUR HEAD OUT OF YOUR ASS!! Now start over!"

There would be two passes, and then "STOP! STOP!!" and the next victim was singled out. The man saw *everything*. There was no safe perimeter while you were in the gym. A player might simply say something to a manager while someone was shooting a free throw at *the other end of the court* and live to regret it. Most of the managers were likewise constantly on edge. We were just as likely to suffer the wrath of Coach Knight if we were not focused. The same went for his coaching staff. Coach Knight was nothing if not fair. *Everyone* was held to the same standard: follow his rules to the letter, or suffer the consequences.

We watched the players deal with the pressure. Fortunately for Indiana Basketball, the players were tougher and more mature than I was. Through all 4 years as manager, there were times when players wanted to quit. There were times when groups of players would feel they were finished, and couldn't take another day, but others would step in and build them back up. Encourage them to hold on. Advise them to trust Coach and follow the plan, and that they could achieve great things. Two weeks later, the roles would be reversed, and it would be the encouragers who needed encouragement. It was rough and it was intense, but those players never thought of fighting among themselves because they all had a common "enemy" to deal with: Coach Knight. In no time, they were a *team*. It was worrisome as a manager to hear the concerns of the players. I would sometimes worry all night about someone who had threatened to quit only to find that all the players seemed to have forgotten about it by the next day. I have, and always will have, the greatest respect for all the players who persevered through the stress, and had, by my senior year, become the best team in the country (despite the loss to Kentucky in the NCAA semi-finals due to Scott May's broken arm).

One other person that earned my utmost respect was Robert M. Knight. Coach Knight was intimidating (I must admit to being scared to death of the man my first two years at Indiana, and never was comfortable when he was around). Coach could also be hilarious. He never cracked a smile when he joked and it was so unexpected that everyone hesitated for a few seconds before laughing, but he could be very funny. He was also one of the most loyal people I have met. He honored and respected the elders of the game who he had learned from, and he was loyal to his former players. Former players were often shocked to hear that Knight held them up as examples to his current team ("Do you think Steve Green would have made that mistake?!"), and would shake their heads in amazement ("I never knew I did *anything* right all four years!"). We managers had the opportunity to see both sides.

In all, I think I learned more of importance from my time as a basketball manager than I did from any other experience in college. A lot of what I learned didn't sink in for several years because I didn't have the experience in life to appreciate what I was seeing. Basically, it boils down to the price that must be paid to achieve excellence: the single-minded determination, the focused effort, and the sacrifice that is *necessary* to be the best. Coach Knight knew what was needed, and pushed the players to the limit to achieve it. Despite the stress and work, I don't think there are any players who would trade that experience for anything, at least the players from the years I was around, when the effort proved so successful. I can't speak for later teams who did not end as successfully, but even those who did not win national recognition, I would hope, realize, now if not then, that they achieved to the limit of their possibilities and that was the true goal.

Looking back, it was apparent that Coach Knight had a firm grasp on knowing what was important, and what was not important. Coach Knight did not only demand excellence on the basketball court, he demanded academic achievement, complete honesty, and strict moral standards.

Others may have the opposite opinion, but I was there, I saw *all* the events, and the results, and I think he was right.

The lessons learned from the experience have helped shape me in later life, but that is not to say I am anything like Coach Knight. In fact, I am, in many ways, the opposite. The lesson is not that one should be strict and unforgiving to others, I do not coach others, but it is that you can achieve almost anything you desire if you pay the price to achieve it; and the price for anything really worthwhile is steep.

When sports fans learn that I worked under Coach Knight in college, there are two questions that almost always come up. First, what was Coach Knight *really* like? I think the closest example I can come up with is George C. Scott's portrayal of George S. Patton in the movie *Patton*. The intensity was never really absent, just sometimes held in check just beneath the surface, and we always felt that we were one small mistake away from suffering the wrath. I finally came to understand that the ultimate effect on me and, I firmly believe, for the vast majority of players, managers, assistant coaches and whoever worked with Coach Knight, was far more positive than negative.

The second question is: was Coach Knight out of control when he was mad, or were his actions just an act? That question certainly came up among those of us involved in the program at the time. Back then I said I simply didn't know, but I think I have a better feel for the answer after the passage of time. Out of control? Seldom, or never. In situations where *he* felt decorum was indicated, his demeanor would be above reproach. He was nothing if not deferential and kind to those who were his teachers and mentors, and those who he felt deserved respect. When he expressed his ideas to people involved in the basketball program "forcefully" he *meant* what he said and he *meant* to say it forcefully. In some of the incidents that raised controversy, where he struck back when someone treated him with disrespect of condescension, he was not out of control; he would argue that he responded the way we all should respond when treated that way. You may disagree with his philosophy and with his approach, but he was neither out of control, nor was it an act. More than most people, Coach Knight simply did not put up a front about what he thought and how he felt. He was himself.

I certainly don't claim that we should all be like Coach Knight. I know that I would not want to live under the stress of that kind of intensity on a daily basis. He would not make a good Secretary of State. On the other hand, if you are in a life or death struggle of some kind, Coach Knight is *exactly* the kind of person you want on your side. He is a natural leader, a first rate intellect, and someone with a hard-core moral foundation. Those are the attributes that stay with those who had the privilege of working with him. With time, the importance of the hard words and harder demands fades, and one remembers the lessons of determination, honor, and devotion. These are lessons that serve one well in life, and ones that often seem to go wanting in today's world. I was fortunate to have been involved in the IU Basketball program and to have worked under Bob Knight. I will always have great respect for Coach Knight and wish him well.

John Charles "Chuck" Swenson

National Sales Representative, Alro Steel
Detroit, Michigan
IU Manager: 1972-1975
Graduate Assistant Coach: 1975-1976
Degree Earned: B.S., Physical Education, Indiana University, 1976

Chuck Swenson is a National Sales Representative with Alro Steel of Detroit Michigan. Previously, Chuck served five years as an assistant basketball coach, and one year as an administrative assistant at the University of Michigan. Prior to that, he served five years as an assistant basketball coach at Penn State University. From 1994-1996 Chuck served as Director of Basketball Operations at Duke University. Chuck also served for seven years as Head Basketball Coach at the College of William and Mary, rebuilding the program and earning recognition as the top performing team in academics in major college basketball. Chuck also served as assistant basketball coach at Duke University from 1980-1987, and the United States Military Academy from 1977-1980. Chuck is married to his wife Betty and has two children.

Chuck Swenson & Coach Knight

Certainly basketball has been a driving force in my life. From meeting Coach Knight at Camp All-America and listening to Coach Clair Bee give clinics, there was never anything I wanted to do with my life outside of basketball. I captained my team in Crystal Lake, Illinois but my scholarship opportunities were few and my career would not have been possible without Coach Knight. It led to a special opportunity to be a manager at Indiana. This led to 28 years as a college basketball coach serving as a Division I assistant and seven as the Head Coach at William & Mary.

I often reminisce about two incidents. After graduation from Indiana, I was looking forward to coaching at the high school level. I went to Coach Knight to ask for advice. It was a decision between Bishop Noll in Hammond, Indiana or Fairview High School in Boulder, Colorado. Coach said, "Where do you think you'd learn more, coaching at some podunk high school or working for me?"

I stated, "Coach, the answer to that is obvious, what do you mean?"

He replied, "Why don't you stay here as a Graduate Assistant Coach?"

I was stunned and said, "Coach, I don't think I have enough experience."

He immediately stated vigorously, "Experience is vastly overrated."

Then I countered with, "As a former manager and no coaching experience, I don't think I will have the players respect."

He barked, "I'll give you a shirt that says Indiana Basketball on it, and that is all the respect you'll need."

I can't count the number of times I told that story when someone asked me how I got into college coaching.

After one year as a graduate assistant, I was working camp, and as I was coaching a station he said, "It's all set. I just talked with Mike Krzyzewski and he wants you at Army. There's just one catch. You have to enlist in the Army." My heart pounded. I had one more year to get my Master's degree. To say I was surprised would be a vast understatement! I stammered something about not being sure about the enlisting part. To which he bellowed, "Do you know what your problem is? You think you're John Wooden. Do you have any idea who else held the enlisted assistant position at Army?" I sheepishly replied, "No, Coach." He replied, "Mike Schuler at Rice, Bob Weltlich at Ole Miss, Dave Bliss at Oklahoma and me. Now do you think you are a better coach that any of us?" Again looking for a hole to climb in, I said, "No, Coach." "Then you should just take it. If you can't get a good job after being at West Point, you should be taken out in a field and shot," he stated authoritatively.

Obviously, I took the job at West Point which led to coaching the JV basketball team, assisting with the varsity and working with Mike Krzyzewski at his alma mater. West Point helped me to learn about leadership, great values, love of country and a unique bonding with my players as I too had been through basic training and military life.

Intimidating? Larger than life? Unrealistic expectations?

Yes, when your eyes met his, the hole that he stared through you seemed like an eternity. I can still see the faces of players on the '76 National Championship team. When I wasn't the target, listening to the tirade was the best entertainment of the day. After all, the words were delivered with passion and intellect and were often quite entertaining.

It would seem to many that Coach Bob Knight would be the least likely candidate to be an encourager. In my opinion, being an encourager is not one that only says positive things, but one who is credible, gains your trust and has balance. Coach Knight had usually built trust through the recruiting process. He had already explained how much he wanted Quinn Buckner or Kent Benson to them by phone, personal mail, or in person visits. Who would buy anything from anybody without the foundation of trust? This trust had been established with convincing discussions of how a player's specific skills were needed and would be developed in the Indiana system. I heard these conversations with Coach Knight listening to him on the phone, copying his heartfelt letters, and in conversations with his assistants.

There were times we all wondered if there was a method to his demand for perfection? Good was not good enough. We were not playing an opponent, but against our own potential. According to Coach we did not know how to push ourselves. We did not know what we were capable of accomplishing. Numerous times he said, "Demand the most of yourself." Or in my case,

"What you know about basketball I could put on the back of a postage stamp." Not always encouraging. But beforehand, Coach had said, "Let me know if I can ever help you." Somehow I knew that he meant it.

Coach Knight's role as an encourager is overlooked by the media or those not living with him on a daily basis or sometimes by simply young men. A compliment from Coach was earned and deserved. He praised behavior he wanted repeated. When he gave praise in front of the team, I felt like I was floating on air. It motivated me to do more, work harder, prepare, and to stay in his good graces. Best of all for me, a compliment made me impervious to any criticism or verbal abuse for a good while. It made me realize I was truly a part of something bigger than myself, even if my role was a small part. The compliment made me realize the standards he set and his expectations for the team and me personally. This form of coaching and encouraging took time and effort on Coach Knight's part.

Mine were not an easy five years, due to being a graduate assistant for just one year. It was never boring and certainly gave me a small glimpse of a man on a mission with a purpose that included me in a small way. He demanded respect in a military way. In fact, it was the proverbial my way or the highway. Still, I had a gut feeling that to quote Bo Schembechler, "Those who stay will be champions." True enough, the 1975 team was 31-1, possessing 8 guys who made the NBA not including one Larry Bird, who earlier dropped out of Indiana.

I found Coach Knight could temper his temper with a willingness to bend and find humor in any setting. After some brutal practices he had the managers bring out 5 gallon drums of Baskin Robbins ice cream. Not to mention Coach Knight's favorite toppings of strawberries, hot fudge, and nuts galore, in ungodly quantities. I can assure you, no one ate more than our demanding and relentless coach. It was produced in a shortened practice. It changed the pace. It made him seem human. The surprise of it all changed the mood. Every day was a classroom for psychology, effort, execution, and fundamentals of the game.

Intensity not only permeated from his face, but in his actions. I witnessed a relentless pursuit of perfection not only on the floor but in the office. He was forgiving of mistakes made in effort or commission, but never omission. He had a unique way of telling you. Whether he did it in a humorous way in front of the team or staff, or a blunt remark you remembered. More important, you responded with more mental effort.

Coach demanded loyalty, but fiercely gave it as well. I heard him on the phone in his office recommending people with superlatives that would mesmerize a lawyer. I often thought that if the person being recommended could just hear the conversation, he would be shocked and eternally grateful. His example inspired me to help former players, coaches and friends in any way that I could. To this day I keep thick files of letters of recommendation based on some of the drafts I had seen him write.

The opportunities which Coach Knight afforded me were numerous as are the fond memories. From observing practice, to office work, to the domination by the 1975 team to the last undefeated 1976 National Championship team, it was a daily clinic. I was amazed at Coach Knight's capacity for work as well as his ability to instill the will to prepare and hunger for excellence in the players and people around him. It was an inexpressibly phenomenal and life-changing opportunity for me. I can never thank Coach Knight enough for the opportunities given to me as a springboard into Division One coaching and life-changing lessons.

Tim "Doak" Walker

Business Manager, Delco Foods
Indianapolis, IN
IU Manager: 1972-1976
Degree Earned: B.A., Telecommunications, Indiana University, 1976

Tim Walker is from Middletown, Ohio, and grew up in a basketball family. His father was the legendary and longtime coach of the Middletown Middies and coached All-time All-American Jerry Lucas in the process of winning five state championships over his career there. Tim came to IU because of the opportunity to be part of the basketball program. After graduation, he spent a brief period working in the athletic department at Indiana University before embarking on a 30 year career in banking and investment services. For the last five years he has enjoyed working with a prominent Italian and specialty food distributor in Indy.

Tim has been married to his wife Cynthia for 33 years and has three terrific and successful adult children and three grandchildren. He still enjoys following the Hoosiers and doesn't hesitate to remind people how great those coaches and players were that built the grand tradition of IU Basketball!

A Journey of Success

When I arrived in Bloomington in the fall of 1972, I had no way of knowing that I was beginning an incredible four-year journey of basketball success. Had that experience been limited alone to the record that Indiana compiled over those four years, most would have considered me fortunate to be part of something like that firsthand. To couple that with the influences from Coach Knight and the lifetime lessons experienced made it a truly unique period in my life.

I grew up in a basketball family in Middletown, Ohio, and in the mid-1950s the threads that would tie me to Indiana Basketball began to be stitched together. Coach Knight grew up playing basketball in Ohio at the same time my father's teams, led by legendary Jerry Lucas, were dominating play in the state. Coach watched my dad's Middies in the state finals in 1956 and later he and Lucas would be Ohio State teammates. As an ardent historian of the game (and with a steel trap memory) Coach Knight would often cite to me players' names and game results from my dad's teams and how he held those teams in high esteem.

Not a gifted athlete, I still loved the game and when it came time to choose a school, Indiana was high on my list. One of the reasons a kid from Ohio would want to attend out of state was the reputation I had always heard of Indiana Basketball (both high school and college). When my father contacted Coach Knight about my interest in serving as a basketball manager, he got a positive reply and that sealed my choice.

So here I was, an 18 year old freshman who was a total basketball junkie, and I was sure I was going to be a big part of a major college program. There would be 4 or 5 managers and I was going to be one of them! Then I got a wake-up call. On my first trip to Assembly Hall I learned there were 13 or 14 managers on staff and, of course, I would be starting at the bottom.

That experience taught me a great lesson that has served me well. The best way to stand out at a job is to do really good work. I took pride in all my tasks, no matter how menial or mundane. Whether it was cleaning up the locker room, pulling tape off the fieldhouse floor, stuffing envelopes for basketball camp, cutting out articles from the newspaper on future opponents, or getting a Coke with ice for Coach Knight after a big win—I did good work. I did have one advantage, Coach knew my name and who I was (not always the case with 14 managers on staff), so I wanted to be sure what he noticed was positive. That whole approach was something I had ingrained in me and it took extra importance because of the higher expectations Coach was putting on the players and staff to be the very best.

The words "play to your potential" and "intensity" may now sound like athletic clichés. When Coach Knight spoke of that in 1972 and '73, it was a different and original concept to many. I have no doubt that he was at the forefront of coaching the game on a mental level that very few were practicing at that time, and that led to much of his success. I truly felt that I had become, even in a small way, a part of a unique team that would soon do great things.

Of course, the conventional wisdom and image of Coach is of his volatility and angry outbursts. When people learn of my time at IU, that's the greatest area of their curiosity. I certainly witnessed my fair share of his temper and even occasionally was the target of his anger. I learned early on to look at myself first or at the message contained in the anger and not focus so much on the vitriol. I realize that is not an easy or popular stance to necessarily take and I will readily admit that, at times, Coach could make a situation worse with his anger. However, make no mistake that Coach Knight was the person that we were following and the person that I knew wanted to lead us to success. I had seen his skill, intelligence, and leadership on many occasions. I was willing to focus on the challenges to overcome, not on the anger. This mindset has helped me time and time again in situations where I might be dealing with a difficult boss, colleague, or difficult problem. A demanding leader is not well received by many in the workforce today. That leader is looked at as being "mean" or "egotistical" by people who say someone is yelling at them. All I can say is, you have no idea what it is like to be yelled at! By putting my ego aside and focusing on the challenge at hand, and listening to those that know more (even when they are negative or critical) I have been able to grow and stay strong and focus on the tasks in front of me.

Finally, Coach frequently spoke of the willingness to prepare as being more important than wanting to win. In many ways my interactions with Coach Knight over those four years were often more like the interactions with a challenging professor as opposed to a basketball coach. If you were assigned a task, you knew you should do it thoroughly and be prepared to defend your decisions thoughtfully. Whether it was making travel plans, solving logistical challenges, planning an event, or working with the other managers on staff, Coach would always quiz me regarding my decisions, choices, and proposed solutions. I learned early on that he often had thought of many solutions and alternatives himself and wanted to know if you had considered them before arriving at a conclusion. He would question you to understand if you understood the dynamics of the problem and to see if your decision would lead to a solution or success. I had to be thorough, detailed, and confident in my explanation and learn not to be intimidated by someone who could easily intimidate. A most valuable lesson.

Those four years were unbelievable; I was at the cusp of a great run of success and watched a great coach be at the pinnacle of his sport. Being a small part of that success is a great source of pride. That experience still influences me to this day, in work and in life, giving me confidence and context to handle almost any situation.

Brad Winters
Writer, Self Employed
Columbus, IN
IU Manager: 1973-1976
Degree Earned: B.S., Physical Education, Indiana University, 1976

Brad Winters is a freelance writer. He specializes in NASCAR and IndyCar racing but capably covers other sports as well. A frequent guest on sports talk shows, his articles have been published in numerous publications, including the popular Chicken Soup series. He is currently working on his first fiction book, as well as writing a non-fiction book on the 1975-1976 Indiana University Basketball team. Brad and his wife, Diane, reside in Columbus, Indiana, and are the parents of seven children and 8 grandchildren. They recently celebrated their 33rd wedding anniversary.

PUKA SHELLS

Prior to the regular 1975-76 season we played the Soviet National Team in a pre-season game at the new Market Square Arena in Indianapolis. I had arrived at Assembly Hall to help get the team on the bus and was planning on driving to Indianapolis with another manager to help at the game. I had my dress clothes in the car but had forgotten a tie and was planning on running by my apartment to get the tie prior to driving to Indy. Minutes before the bus was to leave I was told that I was riding with the team, which had me trying frantically to see if someone had an extra tie to no avail. Knowing how Coach Knight felt about managers dressing up I figured the best I could do, since I did not have a tie, was to wear a puka shell necklace I kept in my sport coat pocket. Kent Benson had bought the necklace as a gift for me when the team played in Hawaii the prior season. Nothing was said prior to the game or after the game about my "new look" so I thought I had squeaked by without Coach saying anything.

The next day at practice the team was still basking in the glory of defeating the Soviet National team handily. Coach Knight was in a great mood and the team had a great practice. When practice was over we were walking back into the locker room and I suddenly felt a finger pressing in my back that was rapidly making its way towards my ribs. I turned around in pain to see Coach Knight, his finger still in my back, with a face that was becoming redder by the second. I suddenly forgot about the pain! His words were simple and loud. "If you ever wear those #@4%$#@43 girl beads again it will be the last time you see your #@$#$%$#@# in Assembly Hall."

It was the last I ever wore them! Still shaking, I drove to my apartment as fast as I could, grabbed the puka shell necklace, and threw it in the dumpster. I bought an extra tie and kept one in each pocket of my sport coat ... just in case.

Nothing was ever said again about the puka shell necklace.

Following the season, Coach Knight was very gracious in thanking me for being a manager. Little did I know then how the time as a manager would impact my life in a positive way every day of my life. I will always be grateful to Coach Knight for the lessons learned. They gave me great memories. They made me a better person.

Kim C. Kohlmeier

Regional Sales Manager, ICS Corporation
Bloomington, IN

IU Manager: 1973-1977

Degree Earned: B.S., School of Public and Environmental Affairs,
Indiana University, 1977

Kim Kohlmeier has enjoyed a career in sales and marketing since his graduation from Indiana University. He has worked for leading national firms such as Cummins Engine Company, Xerox Corporation, HP Products Corporation, and Unisource Corporation. Kim is currently employed by Intelligent Cleaning Systems as a Regional Sales Manager. He has also been avidly involved in Indiana University as an alumnus, and is currently a Vice-President on the Board of the Indiana University I-Men's Association, the university's alumni letter men's club.

A Pleasure and an Honor

As an incoming freshman I was very "proud" to be selected and join the managerial staff to become part of Indiana Basketball, especially showing up with a cast and crutches. To be involved with Coach Knight, great assistant coaches, and the players was a dream come true.

The atmosphere was intense and was always about setting the standards for winning and achievement. These standards were instilled in me and I have set the stage for my career achievements while working for fantastic companies such as Cummins Engine Co., Xerox Corp., HP Products Corp., and Unisource Corp. ... while serving in a variety of capacities.

I thoroughly enjoyed developing friendships with the players, many of whom remain friends today. I was fortunate to sit directly behind Coach Knight on the bench at games and was able to closely observe the interactions between him, the referees and opposing coaches, which proved quite often to be entertaining.

I treasure the friendships developed with my fellow managers as well. We always worked to be accountable, to perform and achieve excellence, striving to meet Coach's expectations—meaning—*no screw-ups*. With Coach Knight I quickly learned everything runs according to plan, like a Swiss watch! I remember talking with other "BIG 10" managers over the years, and they all would be surprised and impressed with the activities we were involved in and assigned.

It was a pleasure and an honor to be a part of INDIANA UNIVERSITY BASKETBALL. I had four wonderful years, developed great friendships, and was part of some of the greatest teams to ever wear an Indiana uniform. Playing for the truly great Coach Knight!

Dan Zweig, CFP

Senior Vice President—Investments, Wells Fargo Advisors, LLC
Fort Wayne, IN
IU Manager: 1973-1976
Degree Earned: B.S., Chemistry, Indiana University, 1978

Dan's major in Chemistry landed him his first job as a Quality Control Supervisor with the US Gypsum Company's Sheetrock plant in Shoals, Indiana. After a year the entrepreneurial bug bit, and led him to a career as a Financial Advisor. He joined A. G. Edwards & Sons in 1981 in his hometown of Fort Wayne, Indiana. Several mergers later the name on the door is now Wells Fargo Advisors. Dan met Beth Rosenberg in 1989 and they married a year later. Two daughters and a son followed, with the oldest now at IU. Dan continues to maintain his IU season basketball tickets, and looks forward to seeing many of you at the games.

Persistent (adjective): Tenaciously Continuing Despite Problems or Difficulties

In the autumn of 1973, Coach Knight was assembling what many feel was one of his greatest teams. You know the names of the players that would eventually win all but one game in two successive seasons and the NCAA Championship in 1976. But as talented as they were a few years later in those tournament runs, they didn't arrive that way as freshmen.

Coach taught many things, but the most valuable just may have been how to be persistent and succeed. And teach he did—not just to those players who went on to glory, but also to a just-turned-18-year-old student manager from Fort Wayne.

As I watched him coach during those October and November weeks when the kinks were being worked out, a player would often seem unable to accomplish a particular pattern or play that Coach wanted him to learn. After a few tries, if the young man couldn't execute the maneuver, Coach would seemingly drop it and move on to something else.

Perhaps he knew of the human mind's ability to work on a problem subconsciously once the problem has been encountered. Then, 20 or 30 minutes later, Coach would come back to the young man and ask him to attempt the play again. More often than not, there was marked improvement, although he'd been practicing something else in the meantime.

Coach's lesson comes back to me on a regular basis. I allot myself one major (tough) crossword puzzle a week: the *Wall Street Journal* Friday crossword, if you want to try it yourself. Invariably, after a few minutes, I will get stuck and can't do any more. I will put it down for a while. I never look anything up. When I come back to it later, several answers will always come to me right away. This process is repeated over a couple of days as I have a chance to pick it up again. By Sunday evening, it's usually done and nearly perfect.

Coach Knight wasn't always known for subtlety, but his understated teaching of persistence has helped me achieve the success I enjoy today.

Thanks, Coach!

Brian Miller, M.S.

Retired educator, administrator and coach, Hamilton Junior/Senior
High School
Hamilton, Indiana

IU Manager: 1974-1978

Degree Earned: B.S., Education, Indiana University, 1978
M.S., Education Indiana University, 1984

In the summer following graduation from Indiana University, Brian Miller accepted a Social Studies and Spanish teaching position at Hamilton, Indiana, Junior / Senior High School. He taught for 33 years, retiring from teaching in June 2011. He served as athletic director from 1980-2006, head track coach from 1979-2008, and again in 2012. Brian also coached cross country from 1984 until his retirement.

The Rest is History

The experience of seeking to become an Indiana University Basketball manager is one that has shaped me profoundly. As a senior at Huntington North High School, I had been the head basketball manager for three years and wanted to continue in that role in college. I mentioned that I was leaning toward going to IU to the father of my girlfriend (now my wife of more than 30 years). He knew the one-time IU Basketball coach Lou Watson from when they had been friendly coaching rivals at the high school level. He said he could contact Coach Watson about how a student becomes a manager at IU although the coach at the time was Bob Knight.

I had mentioned this to some of the players on my high school team. As we were riding the bus to the motel after a season-ending loss in the Saturday afternoon game of the Regional, one of the players asked me in a loud voice if I was ready to move on to be a manager at Indiana. Our coach, Marvin Tudor, overheard and asked me if that was in fact my plan. I said yes, and he volunteered to write a letter to Coach Knight because he had worked at his summer camp. Little did I know that the principal of our high school (Bob Straight – a former great basketball coach himself) was (and still is) a friend of Coach Knight's. Mr. Straight also passed along my name.

I can still recall the day I was sitting in study hall when Coach Tudor brought in the letter on IU letterhead that outlined the procedure for becoming an IU Basketball manager. My dad went with me with letter in hand to Coach Knight's office during freshman orientation and Coach Knight told me to contact the office again once school started in August and the senior manager would contact me. Larry Sherfick did call, and the rest is history. I have come to view this as "playing to your potential" because if I hadn't taken advantage of these contacts, I would not have the memories and experiences that I have today. Throughout my career in education, whether as teacher or coach, I have encouraged kids to take advantage of opportunities, to do their best every day, and just "go for it" whenever they get the chance.

After graduating from IU, loyalty became a valuable lesson that I realized I took away from my experience of working for Coach Knight. As we managers know, if we did things right and worked hard for the program, then Coach was going to help us get jobs after getting our degree. Coach did that for me in the form of a letter of recommendation that helped me get my first teaching position. Through the years we did not have much direct contact, but he got me tickets the few times I requested them and I contributed to the program by participating in the Basketball Scholarship Golf Classic for many years. Coach also showed loyalty to me by accepting my invitation to speak in 1989 at Hamilton High School, where I was athletic director. He turned down the customary check for his appearance, and the evening turned into maybe our biggest single-event fundraiser ever.

Another lesson I learned was anticipation. Just as players have to anticipate moves on offense or defense, managers had to anticipate what was coming up in practice, on road trips, or in games, so things would go smoothly for everyone involved. This was another concept that has served me well in my career in education.

Preparation is a lesson that just rubbed off on me after seeing Coach's organization of practice and putting together a game plan. Working as a teacher and coach for over 30 years, I put those ideas to good use on a daily basis. Some days when I was teacher, coach, athletic director, and parent of young children all at the same time, it was difficult to get everything done on a nightly basis. However, lesson plans and practice plans always took priority. I have coached track and cross country for 34 years now and

I prepare for every practice and meet with the goal of each athlete getting better each day, and spend as much time on preparation whether the team has great athletes or just mediocre talent. Again, my goal is for each kid to do his best every day. At our small school, I still get the equipment around for road trips just like when I was a manager. I'm also the "equipment manager" and do the laundry. I guess once you're a manager, you're always a manager!

Honesty was another lesson that was reinforced while working for Coach Knight. I say reinforced because that is definitely a value that was first instilled in me by my parents. I know there were times, especially as a Senior Manager when Coach and I interacted the most, when players and other managers thought that there would be trouble if they didn't tell Coach what they thought he wanted to hear at a particular moment. I always found that Coach respected honesty, and I have tried to pass that value on to my own kids and my students. I've also let honesty guide me in my dealings with other teachers, coaches, administrators, and members of the community over the years.

My first real job was working at a golf course during summer in high school and for two years of college. In the barn there was a sign that said, "The boss may not always be right, but he is always the boss." Again, the concept of doing what you're told to do by teachers and other adults was inculcated in me by my parents. By the time I got to IU, I had pretty much always adhered to that concept. As I would find out in my four years in the IU Basketball program, those who could accept that idea and did their job as a player or manager stayed. Those who didn't left or were asked to leave. Following that simple tenet has served me well in my professional life in dealing with administrators that I worked under. Just as at IU, sometimes it wasn't easy. However, because of my experiences at IU I probably have dealt with criticism from administrators, parents, the public, etc., better than the average person. Sometimes I thought to myself while listening to some parent rant about how I or another coach didn't treat their kid right that Coach Knight really did prepare us for life. Some of these parents thought they were really getting to me, but inside I knew I had been through much tougher times and could survive about anything they could throw at me. We were in Jacksonville for the Gator Bowl Tournament in December 1977. The Coliseum there was, shall we say, old even by the standards of that era. One of the players was commenting on the condition of the building. Coach Knight told him that this would be good preparation for his future life—in case he went to prison.

The final thing I learned while working for Coach Knight was to savor the special moments. I can still remember standing on the sideline behind Quinn Buckner at the final practice at Assembly Hall before the team left for Philadelphia and the NCAA Final Four in 1976. At the end of the practice, Coach Knight told the team to look around and remember all their accomplishments, and to remember that no one could ever take those away from them. I still use basically the same speech on the rare occasions that one of my athletes qualifies for the State Meet.

I want to salute the senior managers that I worked for: Larry Sherfick, Chuck Swenson, Tim Walker, Kim Kohlmeier, and Russ Bright; my fellow 1978 senior managers Gerry Freitas and Rex Taylor; the "senior" managers for the next two years Dave Skibinski, Pete Schroeder, and John Levenda; and Steve Skoronski who was a freshman when we were seniors. On the rare occasions that we have gotten together and reminisced, it's like we haven't been away at all. The shared experiences bind us together.

Memories and Moments

Years after graduating from IU I attended a basketball alumni golf outing. Former player John Laskowski asked me to tell a story about Coach Knight that nobody would have known about. Las said it would just be between the players and managers. So I told the story about a missing scouting report at the NIT and how Coach Knight was real concerned where it was. It was a Chinese fire-drill but we miraculously found it in two hours in the vast city of New York. I thought it was funny that Coach was so concerned about it because he had the scouting report by that time committed to memory, and we all knew he never forgot anything. When I got my hands on the report I opened up the notebook and discovered a catalog and a letter stating for Coach to pick out a couple pair of golf shoes and they would be sent to him. He wasn't worried about the scouting report—he wanted the golf shoes. During dinner at that outing I was sitting there with some of the guys then all of a sudden a hand came out of nowhere and grabbed my shoulder. It was Coach Knight and he just said—"It wasn't about the shoes." So much for Laskowski keeping a secret—never again.

Being a manager at the start of the Bob Knight era provided many memorable experiences. There was the beginning of the year when we had only 9 players—Coach got that team to a 9-1 record to start the season, beating Kentucky and Adolph Rupp and being ranked number 5 in the country with just a terrible team—because after the first 10 games we lost every game in January, including his first 4 games in the Big Ten. We would look up at the top of Assembly Hall to see if anyone was hanging up there after practice during that month.

Than Lenox

� des des des des des des des des des des des des des des des des

My father passed away a year after I graduated, and I received a poignant letter from Coach Knight. He expressed sympathy on the death of my father and how he persevered after the death of his own father.

John Liston

❋❋❋❋❋❋❋❋❋❋❋❋❋❋❋❋❋❋

During my time at IU the practices were closed. This meant no one other than the team, IU athletic officials, and invited guests should be in the house. One of my jobs was to scour the arena looking for anyone who shouldn't be there. They'd often try to hide themselves in a corner, or wear red to blend in with the seats, but we'd spot them. When approached they knew they shouldn't be there and left without making a scene.

Dan Zweig

❋❋❋❋❋❋❋❋❋❋❋❋❋❋❋❋❋❋❋

The team was going to play an exhibition game at New Castle High School on a Sunday afternoon. This was our first travel situation of the year. In preparation, we held a short practice in Assembly Hall. The plan was to then board the bus for the short drive to the Student Union to have lunch and depart for the scrimmage. It was my responsibility to get the younger players out of the locker room and into the bus to stay on schedule.

The older players knew the drill, the freshmen did not. Coach Knight would use the opportunity to instill into the freshmen the need to be on time. He would simply tell the bus driver to leave when all the older players were on board. I knew we were cutting it close as I hurried the last two players up the stairs. We arrived to see the bus pulling away. Those guys left behind were in a mild panic and were considering jogging after the bus. I quickly got them into my car (1973 Ford Maverick) and we managed to arrive at the Union ahead of the bus. We were waiting at the curb when the door opened and the players and coaches walked out. We fell in with the group and went to lunch. Later that day, Doug Allen, a senior player, told me that as Coach

Knight looked out the bus window and saw us there waiting, he stated: "That manager is just too damned resourceful." To this day, I consider that one of the highest compliments I have ever received.

The Easiest Interview: In 1975 I was interviewing for admission to IU Medical School in Indianapolis. The competition for admission was fierce, and most applicants were on pins and needles throughout the process. You wanted everything in your admission packet to be as strong as possible, including the letters of recommendation. Coach Knight was kind enough (he could be counted on for support like this for anyone involved in the program) to provide a letter of support. I was scheduled to be interviewed by two of the Medical School faculty, and, as one would imagine, was extremely nervous. I needn't have been.

Both faculty members were basketball fans, and the 'interview' consisted entirely of a discussion of IU Basketball and Coach Knight. Indiana had just completed an undefeated regular season, and both the program and Coach Knight had reached national prominence. What questions did I have to answer to determine if I was qualified to become a physician? "What is Coach Knight really like?" and "Does Coach Knight really lose control, or is it an act?" The same questions I had been asked a thousand times.

Easiest interview I ever had.

Todd Woodruff

❆ ❆ ❆ ❆ ❆ ❆ ❆ ❆ ❆ ❆ ❆ ❆ ❆ ❆ ❆ ❆ ❆ ❆ ❆

Thrown Out: Every week, or so, Coach Knight would throw a player out of practice. Whether it was due to insufficient effort, inattention, lack of leadership, or something else needing special emphasis, it would be "Kamstra (or whomever), get the hell off the court! If you don't want to play, go get dressed and get the hell out of here! I don't want to see you here again! NOW GO! GET THE HELL OUT OF MY SIGHT!"

The miscreant would then have to perform the perp-walk to the locker room, presumably to go home; but they had better not actually go home. Early on, one of the assistant coaches would follow the player into the locker room and fill them in on why they were being punished and how to handle it. Eventually, everyone knew the proper procedure.

In five or ten minutes, the banished player would quietly drift back onto the court and join in as if nothing had happened. Sometimes Coach Knight would simply ignore that the player was back, and allow them to resume practice. On other occasions, Coach Knight would yell, "Kamstra! I thought I told you to go home!" in which case the proper response was something like, "Coach, I'm ready to play now," and the incident was resolved.

Out of all the dozens and dozens of instances of players being "thrown out of practice," I don't recall anyone actually leaving Assembly Hall. If it ever happened it was rare, and would have been very negative. Actually, the last thing Coach Knight would want was for someone to miss practice. What he wanted was confirmation that you got the point he was trying to make, and that the player wanted the information he was trying to get across. Over time, we were aware that the players who were thrown out most often were the best players. Coach Knight had higher expectations for them, and demanded more.

Todd Woodruff

✽ ✽ ✽ ✽ ✽ ✽ ✽ ✽ ✽ ✽ ✽ ✽ ✽ ✽ ✽ ✽ ✽ ✽ ✽

Favorite IU Basketball Memory

If I was lucky, I was assigned to sweep the floor. Sweep the floor?? What kind of glamorous job is that?

The answer is—no glamour at all. But it could be glorious!

A lot happens at half-time: The Red Steppers (IU's dance team) might perform. Sometimes there could be a presentation. Then it would be my turn to quickly sweep the floor with those wide dust mops, with the goal of gathering all those stray pom-pom streamers.

If my timing were perfect I would have myself at just the right spot to seemingly lead out "Your Indiana Hoosiers" as team returned to the court and the sound of over 17,000 screaming fans.

In the fantasy of my dreams ... they would be cheering ... for me.

Dan Zweig

❊ ❊ ❊ ❊ ❊ ❊ ❊ ❊ ❊ ❊ ❊ ❊ ❊ ❊ ❊ ❊ ❊ ❊

Bob Knight's first Indiana University Basketball Team in 1971-1972. In the back row, standing, last man on the right is Than Lenox, the first man to serve as Head Manager for Bob Knight at Indiana University.

Photo: Indiana University Archives (P0039923)

1976-1977 Head Managers Kim Kohlmeier and Russell Bright standing courtside during a practice session.

Photo: Indiana University Archives (P0020405)

1977-1978 team photo with former manager, now graduate assistant coach Jack Gabor seated in the last row, second from left.

A treasure for every Indiana Basketball manager, the certificate for being named an Indiana University Letterman. This certificate awarded to Jack Gabor in 1974.

```
                              15 OCTOBER 1965

                                1st PRACTICE

   3:45 - 4:00              FREE SHOOTING

   4:00 - 4:10              THREE LINE LAYUPS

   4:10 - 4:20              FAST BREAK JUMPERS

   4:20 - 4:35              STRAIGHT LANE - WEAVE

   4:35 - 5:25              SCRIMMAGE (Talk)

   5:25 - 5:35              SPEED DRIBBLING

   5:35 - 5:40              FOUR LINE SLIDE

   5:40 - 5:45              HALF COURT SHUFFLE
```

Photo: Courtesy of David Skibinski

One of the rewards for working for Coach Knight was access to interesting people and some of Coach Knight's history. Before leaving campus following graduation in 1980, Coach Knight gave Dave Skibinski access to his personal basketball files. Here is a copy of Coach's first practice schedule as a head coach, from the U.S. Military Academy where he was named head coach at 24 years old.

Head Manager Chuck Swenson sits at the scorer's table (far left), far right is Coach Knight and to his immediate left is team trainer Bob Young. Chuck went on to a distinguished career in college coaching as both an assistant and head coach.

1978 NATIONAL COLLEGIATE
BASKETBALL CHAMPIONSHIP
EAST REGIONAL

On the left, a photo of a room key from the hotel where IU stayed for the 1976 National Championship. On the right, award from 1978 NCAA East Regional Basketball Tournament Champions.

October 13, 1976

Earvin Johnson
814 Middle St.
Lansing, Michigan 48915

Dear Earvin:

I really enjoyed having the opportunity of meeting and talking
with you on Monday. I fully realize you are in a situation where
you can attend school anywhere in the country you would choose.
However, as I mentioned in our conversation, I don't believe there
is a better program for you anywhere in America than right here
in Indiana. Ours is a situation that I think you would thoroughly
enjoy and benefit more from in terms of your progress as a player
than anywhere else. I have met very few people in recruiting that
I enjoyed talking to as much as you. I know we would have an
excellent relationship as player and coach. I would rather have
you come to Indiana than anyone else in the country.

We are really looking forward to having you visit us the 20th-21st
of December. We will be keeping in touch with you and I want to
wish you the very best as practice starts. I have enclosed one of
our basketball brochures from last year I thought you might enjoy
looking through.

Sincerely,

Bob Knight
Basketball Coach

ls

Photo: Courtesy of David Skibinski

Being a manager at Indiana meant you were deep on the inside of most aspects of the program.
Here is a copy of a letter from Coach Knight to a recruit—Earvin Johnson.

MANAGERS MEETING : OCTOBER 12
1977-78 Manager Regulations

I. Practice
   A. Know when you are scheduled, and be there on time.
      1. If conflicts arise, call a Senior Mgr.
         a. We will try to switch practice days with another manager if you must miss
      2. Vacation periods will be discussed later.
   B. Dress Code
      1. Be conservative--please, no patched jeans or strange colors.
      2. Hair--slightly left of the norm.
      3. Dress out for practice unless notified otherwise.
      4. Wear lettered shirts (if you're not dressed out) at your own risk, unless they
say "Indiana University" , etc.
      5. NO moustaches, beards, or sideburns below the earlobe.

II. Managerial Duties (Basic listing)
   A. Before Practice:
      1. Get dressed.
      2. Turn on the lights.
      3. Sweep the floor--don't bitch, just do it!
      4. Place towels, blackboard, and balls on the floor.
      5. Later, place the projector in the locker room.
      6. DO NOT SHOOT while players are on the floor.
      7. Pick up all Zemi cups and loose paper.
      8. Check to see that scoreboard is operable; bring whistles out to scorer's
table.
      9. Fill Zemi tanks and individual water bottles.
      10. Put out "Practice Closed" signs, close gates and curtains.
      11. Run for players' equipment.
   B. During practice
      1. Position yourself along the floor where you can effectively return a ball
to the center of play.
      2. Don't work against each other--you are also part of a team!
      3. DO NOT GROUP TOGETHER with other managers during practice for conversa-
tion's sake.
      4. Be prepared to assist the coaches during drills.
      5. Managers should be seen and not heard--The cardinal rule of managing.
      6. It is the duty of managers to ask unauthorized personnel to leave the Hall.
         a. Be on the lookout for these "undesirables", and if one is spotted, ask
a Senior Manager or an assistant coach if the person is OK, if you aren't
sure.
         b. When asking someone to leave, do it in person (don't shout to him from
the floor), and be polite, explaining why.
      7. Statisticians
         a. Find out what drills you will be keeping stats. for.
         b. Keep your papers in order.
      8. Be on guard for ripoffs!
III. After Practice
   A. Collect balls and count them. (There should be 13).
   B. Return balls, towels, blackboard to the locker room.
   C. Total Stat. Sheets.
   D. Return any of the coaches' equipment to their locker room.
   E. Straighten up players' locker room, and place chairs inside cubicles.
   F. Turn off the lights.
   G. Take equipment upstairs.
   " GO HOME AND STUDY ' '

This is the first of two pages of manager duties and responsibilities for practice sessions for the 1977-1978 season.

Knight's guys finish first

Even when his team is winning, IU coach Bobby Knight grimly paces the sidelines.

The Hoosiers were on the run in 1977 and Head Manager Kim Kohlmeier (immediately to the right of Coach Knight) celebrates with Coach Knight. Typically, the head manager sat directly behind Coach Knight at home games, the ideal spot to see and hear ALL the action.

Photo: Courtesy of Indiana University Archives

The managers of 1974. 1st row: Mark Siegal, Tim Walker, Chuck Swenson. 2nd row: Randy Parr, Dan Zweig, Larry Cannon. 3rd row: Brad Winters, Larry Sherfick, Ed Paternoster. Standing behind: Todd Woodruff.

Photo: Indiana University Archives

The managerial staff of 1976-1977. 1st row: Brad Cummins, Rex Taylor, Marc Goodman, Brian Miller, Russ Bright. 2nd row: John Levenda, David Macer, Dave Skibinski, Gerry Freitas. 3rd row: Kim Kohlmeier, Andy Dean, Pete Schroeder.

Photo: Indiana University Archives (P0045550)

Managers had some of the best seats in the house at Assembly Hall. Here, All-American Scott May goes up for two of his total I,593 points at Indiana. Seated on the bench to the left of May with hands clasped is Tim "Doak" Walker, and on the right with his chin resting on his hand is Gerry Freitas.

Photo: Indiana University Archives (P0030114)

The Hoosiers are jubilant in celebration and 1974 Head Manager, John "Sonny" Liston, is behind the team bench holding a warm-up jacket, with the best view in Assembly Hall.

Classes of
1980-1989

Glen Grunwald, J.D., M.B.A.

Glen Grunwald most recently was general manager of the New York Knicks of the NBA. He previously served as Vice President and General Counsel of the Denver Nuggets, as general manager of the Toronto Raptors from March 1998 until April 2004, and then as President and CEO of the Toronto Board of Trade. Previous to his career with NBA teams Glen was a successful corporate attorney. He has earned a law degree (J.D.) at the Northwestern University School of Law, and a master's degree in business (MBA) from Indiana University.

Born in Chicago, Illinois, Grunwald was a high-school All-American basketball player from East Leyden High School in Franklin Park, Illinois. He is the only player selected All-Chicago area four times, and was player of the year in the state his senior year, 1976. He was injured prior to his freshman year at Indiana University, and although he was a team captain in 1981 when Indiana won the national title, and was drafted by the Boston Celtics in the 5th round of the NBA Draft, he never played professional basketball.

A Player's Perspective

As hard as it is to imagine a world without the proud tradition of IU Basketball and the legend of Coach Bob Knight, that is exactly where we would be without a group of unsung heroes—the managers of his teams. Without them, the great success of the Cream and Crimson would have only been a dream.

Let us not pretend that I can truly speak for all the players who suited up for the Hoosiers in Coach Knight's illustrious 30 year run in Bloomington. That is why it was an honor when Dave Skibinski asked me to provide the IU players' perspective about the team managers who served under Coach Knight. Although each player has had his own unique experience having played on different teams at different times, I believe my experiences and feelings about our indefatigable managers will ring true for all IU players.

If Coach Knight was the driver of the Big Red Machine, and the players were the engine; then the managers had to be the transmission. The managers took all that energy and direction and moved the program forward. Much was asked of both players and managers by Coach Knight ... work hard, go to class and study, attend practice, play by the rules and give your best every day. But the managers' work load did not stop there. Planning transportation and hotels for road trips, preparing and cleaning up after games and practices, attending meetings with coaches, taking and recording stats, filling in as practice players and coaching assistants, helping in the basketball office with administrative work, travelling to pick up coaches, recruits and VIPs, and (before the internet) taping games off of hotel room TV's in faraway locations. And we all know that a manager's to do list did not stop there.

But sometimes, we players were all too oblivious to the efforts and the assistance that our managers provided to the IU Basketball program and to us individually. We were consumed with practices, games, school work and, of course, Coach Knight. Fortunately, our managers were more than willing to enlighten those players who snubbed a manager or, worse, mistreated one. Our managers were not only fully equipped with great work ethic and organizational skill, they also wielded a sharp wit. Players who did not show the proper respect and appreciation to our managers often found themselves cut down a notch or two with a manager's biting remark or humorous practical joke.

But ego was never an issue with our managers. They were working with IU Basketball for all the right reasons. They wanted to contribute to an endeavor that was bigger than them, to be part of team that would compete at the highest level for the biggest prize. Managers didn't receive the accolades or fame of a player, but felt the same sting of Coach Knight's rebukes when their performance didn't meet his high standards. They were the ultimate team players, and to them each player owes sincere gratitude and appreciation.

So, on behalf of the players who were fortunate enough to have played at IU under Coach Knight, we know that we were also blessed to have these managers as our friends and teammates. To them, I say thank you...thank you for a job well done and thank you for your support and friendship.

Pete Schroeder

President, View Outdoor Advertising
Merrillville, IN

IU Manager: 1976 - 1980
Official Scorekeeper: 1981
Degree Earned: B.S., Business, Indiana University, 1980

Pete Schroeder is President and part owner of View Outdoor Advertising. Pete began his advertising career in the winter of 1982 as a sales representative. During the next 16 years Pete rose to the position of Vice President of the Western Region with Whiteco which at that time was the largest independently owned billboard company in the United States.

In 1998 Mr. White sold his sign assets and concentrated on his hotel empire which to date has over 140 properties (including his signature JW Marriott in downtown Indianapolis). Pete went with a start-up sign company as VP of Real Estate until 2005 when he was asked to return to Whiteco and head up Mr. White's newest venture in the advertising business View Outdoor Advertising.

Starting from scratch in a highly regulated business, View Outdoor has been the fastest growing outdoor company in the US. Today with more than 500 advertising signs and over 25 employees, View has offices in Northwest Indiana and downtown Chicago.

Where's the Damn Bus?

Let me explain. Winter 1979. We had just sustained one of the, if not worst road loss in Coach Knight's era at IU: 30 plus points at Minnesota. Interesting how I can vividly recall the events, but struggle with the details! Back in those days without the TV networks running college basketball, Big 10 games were Thursday/Saturday affairs. Travel was set up for the most part so we were not constantly on the road and missed less class time. So here we are, traveling on to Iowa late Thursday night (actually Friday shortly after midnight) and I am anticipating that we would be landing at the Iowa

City (home of the University of Iowa) airport. What a huge error as we were actually landing in Cedar Rapids as the much smaller Iowa City airport was closed during snow season. Unbeknownst to me, that was the plan all along. However I made a huge incorrect assumption as our chartered team bus was waiting for us in Iowa City.

Folks, I was in the major IU manager dog-house for what seemed like an eternity. Let me tell you it was COLD and snowing heavily that late night in Iowa, and we were in the middle of nowhere without a bus or even access to the closed terminal building. Somehow I got in contact with the wife of our bus driver and 2 hours later we were finally picked up. Let me just say for 48 hours I did not want to leave my room. Every time Coach saw me I heard it. At one exchange he said "I should send you back to Bloomington, Patrick (Patrick being Coach's 9 or 10 year old son) could do a better job than you ..." add a little color to the words and that was my life for the next two days.

The last and final exchange went something like this ... "Pete, you're smarter than this and you are an important part of IU Basketball. You just cannot afford to make a mistake like this. You must check and check again to insure accuracy. Be prepared for anything and everything." He also joked about it down the road, saying we always knew when we were getting close to landing when Pete's nose was stuck to the window looking for the damn bus at 10,000 feet.

Let's stay here for a minute. Many people, had they been there, would have thought what a tyrant to treat a 19-20 year old student that way, but let me tell those uninformed people something. That episode is forever etched in my mind and is just one of many examples of life lessons taught that prepared me for a successful career in business. Preparation, accuracy, thoroughness in your job and being a leader are just a few.

Where it began ... for many years my Dad would pick me up after school in Terre Haute and we would drive to Bloomington to cheer on the Hoosiers. We never had a ticket but we were pros at roaming the parking lot and always getting tickets at face value. I loved IU Basketball. In the fall of '76 I walked into the basketball office and was warmly greeted by MaryAnn Davis and announced I wanted to be a manager. A few weeks later after a few meetings,

I had a broom in my hand and was mopping the floor prior to practice. I can honestly say that nearly every day I never lost appreciation for what working within the IU program meant: it was an honor to walk into that locker room and to walk out on that floor. Since then I still hold that near to my heart just as I have an appreciation for hard work. Tough to explain but the old saying, "you had to be there, you had to experience it" holds true.

As a junior beginning the 1978-79 season, I had graduated from mopping the floor to more responsibility and more important, learning the responsibilities that would come with being the senior manager next season. Senior managers have tremendous responsibility in the IU program, including but not limited to scheduling the practice and game-day tasks of the other 8 to 10 managers, but also travelling with the team, scheduling ground transportation, financial record keeping with travel expenses, and ticket requests both home and away. That was my first taste of expect the unexpected. True in August of 1978 and still true today.

Dave Skibinski, a fellow classmate and I were summoned to Coach Knight's office early in 1978 and were told that as Juniors we were going to assume the posts of Head Manager a year early. Were we ready? Did it matter? The point is, looking back, the answers to those two questions are of little importance, no more important than today when faced with a new challenge. We'd figure it out.

Usually on the road we would rent a car so the coaches had transportation. Several times as "keeper of the keys" we would be summoned to the lobby very early in the morning as Coach would need the car—finding out later that these solo trips at the crack of dawn were to go to a local hospital to visit someone. Too early for anyone to see (or report on), he did it for himself and the person he was visiting, and no one else.

One event, to this day, sends chills down my spine. We are on the road, same trip described above. Weather was horrible and I was in the dog-house for the bus snafu. We stayed in that Friday night and were eating dinner in the hotel restaurant with the team. Coaches rarely if ever ate with us on the road. A father approached the table and asked if Coach Knight was here. I informed him that he wasn't, knowing he was in his room with the other coaches looking at game tape. He went on to say that his son loved Coach and had a picture that he wanted to get autographed. I offered to take the picture, try and get it signed, and mail it back to him. He was persistent in a nice way, saying his son and the mother were in the lobby and they would just sit there and see if they could "catch" Coach and meet him.

After dinner I went thru the lobby and there they were ... mom, dad and son who was severely disabled sitting in his wheelchair tightly holding a picture of Coach. Looking back I believe the events I witnessed over the years of Coach doing so much good for people—events outside the watchful eye of the press—prompted me to do something. Remember, Coach is not in a good mood. Bad loss, crappy weather at Iowa, and finally he is really pissed off at me for the bus issue. I said to the father, "Let me see what I can do." I knock on Coach's door. Coach Jim Crews answered and I heard two things ... Crews: "WHAT" and Coach: "WHAT THE HELL DO YOU WANT?" Talking as rapidly as I could, voice shaking, I explained the situation. Coach asks, "Where in the heck are they?" I say in the lobby, and he tells me to go get them. I take them to the room and he visits with them for at least an hour and has me go downstairs and bring them a couple of sandwiches. Folks, that is the Coach Knight I know, and very few people outside the program had the chance to routinely observe!

Today, I owe so much of my success to those four years with Coach Knight. I went to IU as a typical 18 year old, and I left there with such a huge advantage because of my time with Coach. One of my favorite quotes from Coach is: "Everyone has the will to win, but few have the will to prepare to win" has been uttered from my mouth so many times over the last 30 plus years to my employees, to my children and yes to myself. I entered that basketball office in the fall of '76 wanting to be a part of the program, I left there in '80 prepared, so very well prepared, for the rest of my life.

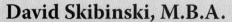

David Skibinski, M.B.A.

President & CEO, SnapMD, Inc.
Los Angeles, CA

IU Manager: 1976-1980

Degrees Earned: B.S. Biology Education, Indiana University, 1980, M.B.A.,
Entrepreneurship, University of Southern California, 1997

Post-graduate studies: Claremont Graduate University

Dave Skibinski is President and CEO of SnapMD, a telemedicine company seeking to transform healthcare delivery in America. He was also co-founder of QuantumMethod, a marketing and communications firm, Intravera Worldwide, a health products company, and a founding shareholder in BioSig, a cardiac healthcare company. Dave has been in the healthcare field for over 25 years; previously he was with GlaxoSmithKline and Dendrite International in sales and marketing management roles. Before his career in business, Skibinski served as an assistant basketball coach at the University of Evansville and the U.S. Military Academy, where he was also a member of the faculty. Dave holds a Bachelor of Science degree in Biology Education from Indiana University and an MBA from the University of Southern California. He was married for twenty-one years to the late Annie Johnston Skibinski.

A Long Road from Hammond

When John Bobalik cut me from the freshman basketball team at Bishop Noll Institute, he set me off on a journey I could not have predicted. I went on to run our school's training room and equipment room, and even had the opportunity to be a ball boy and training room assistant with the New England Patriots. My love for basketball never faltered. I was just too small and lacking athletic ability, especially in my early high school years. But Providence can be a powerful force in life and all those wonderful high school experiences were part of the packet I sent to Coach Knight asking to be considered as a manager with Indiana Basketball.

One of my prize possessions is the letter I received from Coach telling me to report to the basketball office when I arrived on campus to begin my freshman year at IU. My first contacts with Indiana Basketball were with Coach Knight's Administrative Assistant MaryAnn Davis who was very welcoming, and I was later introduced to Assistant Basketball Coach Tom Miller. Coach Miller welcomed me to IU Basketball, asked me a handful of questions and put me in touch with the head managers who did a thorough interview. Needless to say, I was thrilled to get the call that I had been selected to be a manager.

Create an Environment of Success

Coming from Northern Indiana, and a family of modest means, I had never seen an Indiana game in person, so it was quite a shock on the first full day of practice to not only be in Assembly Hall but to be on the court and see Coach Knight for the first time. I can recall the diligent atmosphere in Assembly Hall as the players entered the court for pre-practice drills, but I *really* recall how the intensity climbed as Coach Knight entered the arena and practice began. There was no dead time, no quiet time to explain drills. He would bark instructions and as he finished, the ball was in play—the tempo was intense and you had to learn on the run.

From those earliest days I learned the value of time, and how to create an atmosphere for success. In everything we experienced at Indiana, there was a purpose, and it was planned. There were patterns to practice, pre-game preparation, everything we did. I learned to listen for the way Coach opened the gates and curtains that led onto the court and I could predict somewhat reliably how practice might go. I also watched how he routinely entered the locker room on game day, laying his sports coat across a laundry basket, and went to the blackboard and wrote down the numbers of our opponent's starters, and diagonally wrote across those numbers the name of our player who would guard them. On occasion, a special occasion, Coach would break that pattern, and without saying a word you could feel it was a special moment, and you had better be ready. And at the start of the year, we had a board in the locker room that had our metrics for success—the key stats that would define our chance to win.

In my professional life as a manager of sales teams, I applied those lessons of creating an environment of success, a place where people know what is expected, and want to achieve beyond even their own expectations. At the start of every year as a sales manager, I held a meeting to define our metrics for success, and strove to create an environment for superior achievement. Fortunately, I recruited good teams that achieved great success.

Know Your Friends

During the winter of my freshman season I learned another lifelong lesson. That was not an easy time for IU Basketball. 1976 featured the last college basketball team to go undefeated. The team of 1977 featured one returning starter, Kent Benson, and six freshmen. Midway through the season the team was tired. Practice was not going well and at one point Coach had the team sit on the court as he sat atop one of the large foam cushions below the south basket of Assembly Hall. Coach then spoke to the team, especially the freshmen, about the expectations of being an Indiana Basketball player—the responsibilities to the State of Indiana, the University, the Team and, most important, yourself. He spoke about friendship, and the need to distinguish between friends and acquaintances. He told the players that because of their position on Indiana Basketball team, there would be people who would try to take advantage, and that they had to recognize they were part of something bigger than themselves. I still can hear his words. He said most people are lucky if they have two handfuls of true friends, and for most, it was more likely, one hand's worth. Over the years I have developed my own criteria for friendship, and when I count, I feel fortunate to have two hand's worth.

Respect the Past

I also recall the spring of 1979 for many reasons. It was a tough year for Indiana Basketball. Coach had dismissed a few players from the team. We struggled through the Big Ten but were awarded a spot in the National Invitational Tournament—NIT. To start the tournament we went down to Lubbock, Texas, to take on Texas Tech. The Lubbock Municipal Coliseum was sold out and raucous that night; streamers a foot thick circled the court before game time—it seemed a setting ripe for an upset. But our players rose to the occasion and handily defeated Texas Tech and we proceeded through the tournament to earn a spot in the finals in New York City. A day or two before we were to leave for New York, Coach called me over at the start of practice and instructed me to go to the university bookstore and prepare several identical boxes of the "best IU logo merchandise." As we prepared to go to New York Coach instructed me to ensure those boxes went with us to

New York. Upon arrival in New York we went to Madison Square Garden to practice. As practice proceeded, Coach asked us to bring in the boxes of IU gear. He methodically presented each box to a group of old coaches and supporters that were gathered with him in the Garden that night. They all grinned from ear to ear to be remembered so kindly by Coach Knight. Years later, when I was coaching at West Point, my boss Pete Gaudet, would take me to the Metropolitan Coaches Association gathering prior to the start of the season. There I was standing with Billy Raftery, Lou Carnesecca, and other luminaries of college basketball, and I was welcomed with open arms when they learned I was from West Point and had worked for Coach Knight. While my parents had previously taught me to respect my elders, those two experiences taught me the importance of treating others well, and remembering where you came from. I was riding on a very long tail from Coach's years at West Point some 20 years earlier.

Tenets of Management

It may come as a surprise to some that Coach Knight delegated a tremendous amount of responsibility to those around him. My peers and I over the years handled tens of thousands of dollars from Indiana University to pay for road trip expenses. We arranged hotel spaces, practice facilities, team meals, managed the film exchange, and more. But as much responsibility as we were given, we were held equally accountable. Just as the players were expected to execute on the court, we were expected to execute behind the scenes. From all these experiences I learned from Coach Knight the basic tenets of management: 1) Set clear and realistic expectations; 2) Describe how performance will be measured; 3) Provide adequate resources to get the job done; 4) Provide timely feedback and adequate direction to improve performance. While working for Coach Knight, you always knew what was expected, he ensured we were equipped for success, and, yes, we got feedback on our performance. In its simplest form, none of us wanted to let down Coach Knight, the team or our peers. That esprit de corps never failed.

Fair, Not Equal

Michael Woodson is one of my favorite Indiana Basketball players of all time. Woody was a class act from Day 1. He treated everyone well, was always on time, worked diligently, and always said thank you. You knew he came from a good home just by meeting him. He also happened to be the top scorer during my time as a manager. And to be a top scorer, you have to take more shots than your teammates. Coach Knight continually reinforced to the team the fair, not equal doctrine, that basketball was not an equal opportunity game. Woody could take more shots because it was fair as he would make the majority of those shots, while others on the team would not. It would not have made sense for all the team members to take an equal number of shots; our won – lost record would definitely have suffered. When I became a sales manager, I always kept this in mind when I was allocating promotional budgets. Some sales territories could generate more sales for certain products, and those territories deserved a larger allocation of resources. It was fair, but not equal.

The Long Grey Line

I am fortunate to have followed in Coach Knight's foot-steps to be an assistant coach at West Point, just as Chuck Swenson had several years before me. It was a great experience as I was surrounded by some of the finest young people in America. Coach Knight introduced me to one of his former players, Army head coach Mike Krzyzewski, and his assistant, Pete Gaudet, during the 1980 NCAA Finals in Indianapolis. Shortly after Coach "K" became head coach at Duke, and after Pete was named Army's new head basketball coach, I was hired by him as an assistant. Having spent five years at the Academy I often wondered how much of Coach's philosophy was molded by his time there, and his love of military history. While at West Point I often read the inscriptions on statues of the likes of George Patton and Douglas MacArthur, hearing in my head Coach Knight's voice echoing their mighty words.

Coach, thanks for all the lessons learned with you at Indiana, and for your confidence then and now.

Chris Stone, M.A.

President, Greenville Convention & Visitors Bureau
Greenville, South Carolina

Sports Information Office Student Intern: 1977

IU Manager: 1978-80

Degrees Earned: B.A., Telecommunications, Indiana University 1980
M.A., Sports Administration, Ohio University 1981

Stone is an accomplished expert in the travel industry. His ambitious work is centered on creating high quality destinations by merging design, architecture, and authentic experiences. He's most noted for remarkable achievements in the urban context of Greenville, South Carolina.

Stone's passion for extraordinary visions have teamed him alongside the world's leading architects, planners, and designers. Stone is a frequent speaker and has consulted with a variety of destinations on visitor product development and experience related topics.

He's presented at Harvard's Graduate School of Design; authored destination recommendations regarding Northern California's Monterey Peninsula to the Packard Foundation; and most recently for the European Union's Cultural Consortium, provided evaluation of six visitor serving attractions in Rome, Barcelona, and Paris.

Chris has twenty years of destination experience, serving in senior executive roles in Austin, Texas; Portland, Oregon; St. Louis, Missouri; and Washington DC. He and his wife Sandra have two daughters.

The Class That Never Dismissed

If you took the time to sift through the course listings at Indiana University back in the late 70's, you'd never find the class that had the most profound and enduring effect on my life and career. This class was limited in size, had no formal title, offered no syllabus and required no final exam. The teacher was Coach Bob Knight. And the entire curriculum was built around one word: Excellence!

My passion for sports first led me to be a student intern for the IU sports information office. That initiation gave me insight and connections to a wide range of IU athletics, and built my enthusiasm for a career in sports administration. Having been a high school basketball player, the lure of working with the IU Basketball team turned out to be the opportunity of a lifetime!

It wasn't just the basketball that drew me to the position; it was a recognition that this program was a collection of exceptional people doing remarkable things. In the world of college basketball, this was a Fortune 100 company. The best of the best. And at the helm stood a legendary figure: charismatic, endearing, and laser focused on success. Coach Knight's reputation was as a highly successful leader of men, and I knew there were lessons to be learned that would serve me well.

My first responsibility was to help videotape practice. I dove right in and worked hard to capture every detail. After a few days, I was introduced to Coach Knight, who informed me that while he appreciated the work, he was looking for more of an "executive summary" then he was a hardwood version of "War and Peace." His directive was clear, and he ended our chat with a pat on the back and words of gratitude and encouragement. Knight had a specific need, communicated precisely what he wanted, recognized my youth, inexperience and effort, and encouraged me to perform at a higher level. And I did. Lesson learned.

Looking back it makes me laugh at the range and magnitude of the manager duties, especially those performed "off the practice floor."

- Hours of hand-clipping "bulletin board" trash talk from opposing team hometown newspapers.

- Driving far enough to pick up television reception for an opponent's game ... checking into a hotel ... videotaping the game, then returning to Bloomington (my best trip was being snowed in at Kenosha, Wisconsin for two days ... lots of Brats!). Back then, the thought never occurred to me how creepy this seems today!

- Constantly being asked by assistant coaches, "Hey, how do you spell Isiah's name?"...to this day, whenever I see him, I spell out his name in my mind. I - S - I - A - H! Forever etched.

🏀 Being tall enough at 6' 3" to sign autographs alongside the players.

🏀 For 1979 Pan American Games player Ralph Sampson ... driving to Indy to pick up his specially made gargantuan shoes.

🏀 Washing team uniforms at a New York City urban laundromat for the NIT championship game (over Purdue!), with no patrons paying us any attention (Hey, we're here washing Indiana University player uniforms ... Aren't you interested????).

I rubbed elbows with some of the college game's best and most celebrated players and coaches, met celebrities and legends, traveled what felt like a million miles, and loved every second of it.

But more than anything else, I learned.

I learned that there is nothing more fun than achieving the highest level of success while competing against the highest level of competition. And that achieving success doesn't happen by chance. Instead, it is the result of tireless preparation, unflinching focus, and pure effort.

I learned that leading isn't easy. Coach Knight ran the program with crystal clear and uncompromising expectations of extraordinary effort on the part of everyone involved—including himself. The thing that seemed to frustrate him most was inconsistent effort or a failure to demand the most of yourself. So he developed, cultivated and protected a culture of excellence and high performance. If you bought in and gave your best, success was usually in hand. Excellence rarely tolerates compromise.

I learned that nothing feels more rewarding than hard-won praise. That reaching a goal is an opportunity to set an even higher goal. That the most important parts of leading are setting clear goals, establishing clear expectations, mandating accountability and then empowering your people with the tools, support, and opportunities to achieve excellence. And that it takes talent, experience, and an unyielding will to succeed to achieve true excellence.

Now, more than 30 years later, those lessons I learned echo across my life like Coach Knight's voice across the practice floor. I find myself striving for excellence in all that I do, and encouraging those around me to do the same. I lead by example, as I was taught to do. I empower those around me to succeed, and provide them the tools, support and opportunities to do just that. And I strive to surround myself with the best of the best – people who understand the vision of excellence and are willing to do what it takes to achieve it.

When I do stop and look back on my days at Indiana, it is with fondness, gratitude, and a smile. And when I speak of my years at the University, and my experiences with Coach Knight, it is with a pride and appreciation.

Just a few weeks ago, I was asked what grade I thought Coach Knight would give me in evaluating my career. My answer? "He'd pat me on the back, give me a solid B, and send me off to figure out how to make it an A."

Coach, I'm still striving for my best!

Steve Skoronski, J.D.

Health Care Supply Chain Consultant
Kohler, Wisconsin

IU Manager: 1977-1981

Graduate Assistant: 1981-1984

Degrees Earned: B.S., Accounting, Indiana University, 1981
J.D., Law, Indiana University, 1984

Steve Skoronski is a health care supply chain consultant after being the CEO for 13 years and owner of a medical supply distribution business, Associated Medical Products, Inc. Associated was based in Indianapolis and had eight distribution centers across the country and over 110 employees at the time of its sale in 2004. Skoronski also currently serves on the board of directors of a retirement community in the Milwaukee area and the Boys & Girls Clubs of Sheboygan County, Wisconsin.

Skoronski began his professional career as an attorney with the law firm, Schottenstein, Zox & Dunn in Columbus, Ohio. From there he entered the financial world as a Vice President of Canadian Imperial Bank of Commerce in the U.S. Capital Markets Group and later joined Bando McGlocklin Capital, a small business investment corporation, as a Vice President. Skoronski formed a group of investors that purchased the companies that became Associated Medical Products in 1991.

Skoronski currently lives in Kohler, Wisconsin, with his wife of 25 years, Amy.

At Indiana ... Everybody Hustles

Few people can say they made one of the best decisions of their lives when they were 17 or 18 years old. But like about a hundred or so other young men who were student managers for Indiana University Men's Basketball teams coached by Bob Knight, I can. Outside of my parents, nothing did more to shape the person I became than my experience working for Coach Knight. Seven years of undergraduate and law school education, while valuable, did not teach me as much as I learned in Assembly Hall and various other locations across the country.

While I can recall without effort the basics of accounting and principles of law learned sitting in classrooms in Bloomington, Indiana, it is a struggle to put faces and names on those who led the lessons and those who sat with me. It is also a struggle to say how much those lessons actually helped me after leaving Bloomington. However, I vividly recall the first practice I worked for Coach Knight. He summoned me, and then he got after me as only he could, because I was walking toward him—rather than running. I can picture players, smiling at my expense—and the older managers, stone-faced because they likely had a similar experience. The lesson was learned quickly and with lifelong impact: If you're part of a team, everybody hustles and everybody hustles all of the time. There were other lessons via real-life experience in personnel management, resource allocation, functioning in high-pressure situations, character building, and integrity. Sure, such things were being taught in the School of Business or the School of Law—but not half as effectively as they were in Assembly Hall.

I played football and ran track in high school. I was just good enough to be on teams and compete, but certainly not good enough to play at a higher level. Being a manager at IU, you could, in a way, be on the team. We worked hard, kept our heads down, our mouths shut, and did lots of tasks that don't appeal to many teenagers or young adults. I think we became young adults a lot faster than our classmates. Our role on the team forced that transition. It's been said of many behind-the-scenes roles that you notice them only when they fail. The success enjoyed by IU Basketball in the Bob Knight era and the fact that even the biggest fans can't remember any of us managers is testimony to how well we did. And we did a lot.

So what sticks out the most? For me, it's Coach Knight's basic principle about developing in his players *the will to prepare to win.* He often mentioned that everybody wants to win and that the will to win is one of the most overused phrases in sports and everything else. To him, the will to win was nothing unless accompanied by the will to prepare to win. What we did as managers was not only important in the team preparing to win but taught us how to prepare as well. It was never enough to think for the moment. We always had to be thinking about what was next. The next practice, the next game, the next road trip were always on your mind as a manager. If they weren't, your contribution would be diminished, if not actually harmful to the team effort.

Two road trips my senior year illustrate this point. The first of these trips was our Christmas-break trip to Hawaii in December 1980. At that time, senior managers made sure the logistics of each trip were executed properly. Athletic department and basketball office staff made hotel reservations and travel arrangements before the season, but the managers made sure that actual travel went as planned. There may have been a contract for a bus company to meet the team at an airport, but in the days leading up to the actual trip we would make several calls to that company to make sure the bus they sent would be appropriate for us and, critically, that it would be there no matter when we might arrive. For this Hawaii trip, an assistant coach informed us he would handle all of our regular travel duties because it was such a long and fairly complicated trip. We managers could sense danger in the air.

The trip got off to a pretty inauspicious start—or rather it almost did. We had just returned from a difficult road loss to North Carolina in Chapel Hill, the team we later beat in Philadelphia for the National Championship. Coach Knight was extremely frustrated with the team's play and he told the team that we weren't going to Hawaii unless he could see that things would change. Our plan was to leave for Manhattan, Kansas, to play Kansas State, and then travel from there to Chicago to catch a flight to Honolulu. We had about 25 people in our traveling group, so this was going to be a good test of what we had learned to that point in our careers. Even though Coach said we weren't going to go, we couldn't very well not prepare for this trip, especially since there was only a day or so to do so. So we went ahead with our preparations, assuming it would get worked out, but we couldn't let it be seen that we thought Coach Knight wasn't serious in his position. We had the players and coaches bring their bags in well before practice and we stored them along with all of the other travel gear in the small dressing rooms that are off the hallway connecting the locker room to the training room. After several very long team meetings, things were resolved and we left for Kansas State—hours behind schedule, but everything was at the ready when we got the word.

At that time the senior managers always carried the travel funds and handled the tickets. Gary Sims, my fellow senior manager, handled the tickets and I was responsible for the travel funds. For most road trips we took several hundred dollars. For the Hawaii trip, I went to a bank in Bloomington and cashed a $15,000 check from the athletic department. Most of this was in traveler's checks which took me about two hours to sign. I kept the money in a briefcase that never left my sight. We spent less than half the money, but I was personally responsible for every penny. A university credit card would have saved an awful lot of worry, but in those days that wasn't an option.

The team responded well to Coach's challenge. We beat a really good Kansas State team led by future NBA All-Star Rolando Blackman on their floor, 51-44. Though we left the next day in a blizzard, the trip to Hawaii was actually pretty smooth. Upon landing in Hawaii, we learned the assistant coach handling the trip had not done what we would have done. The bus that met us at the Honolulu airport was one of those small school buses that had a stated seating capacity of about 30. Technically, it was big enough to seat 30 people—but not 30 really big people with a lot of luggage. Seeing this situation, Coach Knight pulled aside Gary, me, and Pete Schroeder —our graduate assistant who had been a senior manager the year before. He told us to get the group out of there. We knew we had to get better transportation and to get ahead of the team to our hotel to see what else needed to be smoothed out. Gary stayed with the team and got all of the luggage rounded up and loaded on the school bus. Pete took several hundred dollars and flagged down a coach bus that was dropping off a tour group and talked the driver into picking up our group. I approached a man who was dropping someone off at the airport and talked him into giving me a ride out to our hotel, a resort on the north end of Oahu. I am sure I paid him. I don't remember how much, but I am pretty sure I got a receipt.

At the hotel, I informed the front-desk clerk that I was with the Indiana Basketball team and wanted to go through the arrangements for our stay. He did this and mentioned that everything should be ready for our arrival the next day. I think he was more panicked than I was when I told him that the team was right behind me and would be arriving shortly. He got the manager and we feverishly worked to get things straightened out. The three of us handed out room keys to our guys as they walked off the bus.

Pete, Gary and I pretty much had to rework the entire trip—except for the games, which in the short run did not go very well as we lost 2 of 3. In the long run, this was just another part of the journey of our national championship season. Best of all, I don't think any of the players ever noticed that this trip was different from any other.

The other road trip that stands out was to Minnesota in January 1981. We always had a staff of about 12 or so managers, and at least 4 or 5 guys would either fly or drive to games. But because of the distance and some recent restrictions on driving, Coach Knight said that only I would go on this trip. This would have been completely overwhelming except for a couple of things. First, I was prepared. It was my fourth year and I had handled all of the various manager responsibilities. So there would be nothing new—unless a problem came up, but I had experience with that as well. Second, even though I was the only manager on the trip, I was part of the team. The players and coaches knew I was alone and they pitched in and did some things managers ordinarily would have done.

The game itself was a tremendous learning experience. Minnesota had always been very talented and this team—with future NBA stars Randy Breuer and Trent Tucker—was no different. We were down at halftime by about 10 points. In the locker room Coach Knight went to the chalkboard and diagrammed one play. He asked every guy if he understood. He drew it out over and over. The chalk crumbled from his emphasis. He told the team this one play was all we were going to do in the second half. He didn't care if we lost by 50 points, we were going to run only this play. Anyone who didn't run this play correctly was coming out of the game and wouldn't return. The half opened slowly for us, with a few substitutions as it began to sink in that Coach really wanted only the one play. As guys started to see the play would work if they executed well, our performance improved to the point where we tied the game in regulation and won in overtime. It was a great lesson in mastering the basics, persevering with a plan, and executing it really well.

After the game, a few of the players and Brad Bomba, our team doctor, helped me get everything packed up. There wasn't room for me on the team plane so I was taking a commercial flight back to Bloomington the next day. As the team boarded the bus to the airport, Coach Knight stopped to make sure I was set for my trip home. He slapped me on the back of my shoulder, just as he did anybody else on the team when he did well, just as we were taught.

Although being a manager meant a lot of hard work, long hours and little public reward, I would not have traded the experience for anything. Coach Knight is one of the most interesting people in sports -and American culture—in the last 40 years. Every manager can say Coach Knight is a decent man and that we benefited from the years spent working for him. No matter which years we worked, we all met guys who became legends in a legendary college basketball program. In many cases those guys were and still are our friends. And I doubt any of us can forget the excitement that went everywhere the team did and the roar of the crowds, especially in Assembly Hall. We knew the excitement and the roar were for Coach Knight and the players. But we were part of the team, so maybe just a little was for us, too.

Gary D. Sims, M.S.

Science Teacher and Varsity Girls Basketball Coach
Edgewood High School
Ellettsville, IN

IU Manager: 1978-1982

Degrees Earned: B.S., Health and Safety / Biology
Secondary Education, 1982
M.S., Secondary Education IUPUI, 1989

Gary Sims began his teaching and coaching career in 1982 at Morristown High School in Morristown, Indiana. He served as a biology and human anatomy teacher while coaching a variety of sports. After seven years he moved to Mitchell High School and continued a career as a biology teacher and basketball coach. He coached the boys' varsity at Mitchell for 9 years, including winning the last single class sectional in 1997. After spending 18 years teaching at Mitchell, he relocated to Edgewood High School where he currently teaches biology and human anatomy as well as coaches the girls' varsity basketball team. In his five years at Edgewood, his teams have averaged 16 wins and he has led them to the Elite Eight twice. He has been married to his wife Kimberly for 30 years and they have one son, Jason, and daughter-in-law Shannon.

Bigger Than Basketball

I suppose as a high school basketball coach, first with boys and currently with girls, that I should share what I was able to glean from Coach Knight from a basketball view point during my time as an IU manager. Certainly, there are practice drills and game preparation that I use or have used that came from my experience at Indiana. After all, whether boys or girls, basketball is basketball. There are a number of former IU managers who went into coaching, at all levels, from the NBA to high school. Coach's influence on basketball is well known and well regarded, so I will assume that is just a given.

I knew Coach Knight always went out of his way to help people, but I never knew, and never will know, how much. Who knows how much he has done to help me? Who he spoke with, who he called? And, as I was able to observe, you didn't have to be directly associated with the basketball team to share in his generosity.

One year during our annual road trip to Northwestern, as we were practicing in the Northwestern field house, Coach asked me to call a local hospital to see if a particular woman was still a patient there. I do not know if he went to the hospital after the workout or even if he called her, I just know he wanted to provide encouragement to this person. That is when I recognized that the most important part of coaching is not simply how many games you win (still important!) but how you help those around you. Coach taught me that there is high value in using your position and influence to help others, and that you don't do it for public recognition.

I have heard Coach say on a number of occasions that if you want to be liked by everybody, stay out of coaching. Whew, this is so true! I am glad I had a heads up on this going into the profession. A high school basketball coaching job in Indiana is a very recognizable and criticized position, and even more so in a smaller community. Let's just say that people can be "somewhat passionate" about their local team. In smaller communities, you as a coach are one of the more recognizable individuals. You are the discussion at Saturday morning breakfasts, phone calls to the athletic director, and yes, even during Sunday school. I found that your critics can find ways to discredit you, even with lies and half-truths. Coach Knight certainly faced this on a much grander scale. But in my four years at Indiana, one thing always rang true. Coach Knight always remained steadfast to the task at hand and, more important, always took time to reach out to help a variety of individuals, no matter what criticism he was currently facing. I have appreciated seeing this firsthand, and have always tried to do the same, in spite of how some people may have viewed me as a coach based on my team's performance.

Being a part of Indiana Basketball is something for which I am forever grateful. I own a National Championship ring, thanks to the great tournament run of the team in 1981. I shared awesome moments with the teams and my fellow managers. I was able to observe daily the sheer effort (our players worked HARD) of our team. I sat in on film sessions and team meetings. I helped out in drills and refereed scrimmages. I arranged bus transportation and handled finances on the road. Yes, it was more than just filling water bottles, although I would have done only that if it meant the same experiences. Every manager has his own stories and memories. Who wouldn't while working for someone like Coach Knight? I am thankful that I had a role, small as it may have been, in the tradition and history of Indiana Basketball.

Mike Agee, M.S.

Vice President of Marketing, Bob Evans Farms Inc.
Columbus, Ohio
IU Manager: 1979-1983
Degrees Earned: B.S., Business Administration, Indiana University, 1983
M.S., Sports Administration, Ohio University, 1986

Mike Agee is vice president of marketing, Bob Evans Farms Inc. Bob Evans owns and operates more than 560 family restaurants in 19 states. In this role, Mike is responsible for all marketing initiatives to ensure continued growth, expansion and customer loyalty. Prior to joining Bob Evans, Mike served in various marketing leadership roles at Procter & Gamble, Red Roof Inns and Exel.

Mike has been married to his wife, Dorice (also an IU grad), for 28 years. They have three daughters: Lauren (23), Haley (21) and Adrienne (18). In his free time, Mike has run more than a dozen marathons and he is an active Christian. He has participated in a number of mission trips to Central and South America, and completed various prison and youth/children's ministry programs.

Perspective

Throughout 1979 to 1983, I had some of the most enviable perspectivesof Indiana Basketball. During the past 30 years, my perspective on my time in Bloomington has never wavered from how fortunate I was to experience it all.

Perspective (noun): the appearance to the eye of objects in respect to their relative distance and positions

I grew up in Terre Haute, Indiana, which is about 60 miles west/northwest of Bloomington. As with many boys in the state at the time, I grew up bleeding Hoosier red. Indiana Basketball wasn't bigger than life—it was life. And it was something that I wanted to be my life.

My perspective got closer when I was fortunate to play both basketball and golf at Terre Haute North for Mr. Howard Sharp, who went on to become an Indiana high school coaching legend from his success at Terre Haute Gerstmeyer High School. Mr. Sharpe won 724 games in his 47-year career, and my up close perspective as a player on his squad introduced me to what Indiana Basketball was all about: discipline. We had to get our hair cut, wear our socks a certain way, and dress in shirts and ties for home and away games, among other things. Little did I know that Mr. Sharp was preparing me for the rest of my life, and thanks to him, I had the opportunity to find out what discipline meant as part of the Indiana University men's basketball team.

As a freshman manager, I didn't personally interact with Coach Knight all that much. Interaction was a rite of passage. My perspective of him was close enough that I quickly began to absorb lessons and insights that would play an important role for the rest of my life. For example, I recall early in my freshman year becoming exposed to Coach Knight's definition of discipline: Doing what has to be done when it has to be done. Doing it the best way you possibly can, doing it that way every time.

I've never forgotten that definition. There aren't too many weeks that go by when I don't think about discipline and how it can positively impact my personal and professional life. Discipline isn't a choice in my life today because discipline wasn't a choice in my life then. If you were in, you were all in. I witnessed firsthand the benefits of discipline in how we taped basketball games, ran drills, prepared for games, and attracted the best people to be affiliated with the program. My responsibilities today are far different, but I know that if I'm involved in anything, I'm all in.

Naturally, my perspective to Coach Knight grew closer during my time affiliated with Indiana Basketball. I ran elements of his summer camp for high school coaches and youth players. I participated in pre-season conditioning runs and officiated team scrimmages with the players. I watched games from the end of his bench. As one of the senior managers, I sat at center court as the official scorekeeper. I saw it all from perspectives that many could only dream. And yet, I never dreamed that Coach Knight saw me from his perspective. How could he? His priorities were much bigger than a manager's. His team was number one in the country. He was playing for Big Ten and national championships.

An experience my senior year reminded me that no matter the level of Coach Knight's daily interaction with me—or any member of his program—he always knew what you were doing if you were associated with Indiana Basketball. I was working in the coaches' locker room taking care of my responsibilities when Coach Knight walked out of the shower and right toward me with a towel around his waist. He sits down asks something along the lines of, "How's it going, Mike? Let's talk for a little bit. What's going on in class? I see you are in J401. What are you reading in that class?" I told him we were reading *The Prince*, which was a political treatise by Italian diplomat, historian and political theorist Niccolò Machiavelli. Coach Knight went on to tell me that *The Prince* was one of his favorite books and proceeded to correct me on a fact about the book's contents. It always struck me that he knew the class I was taking, he knew my professor, and he was so well read.

So there I was with arguably too close a perspective to a naked Coach Knight when I had one of my most profound memories of my time affiliated with his program. As a leader, he didn't just know everyone. He knew everything about everyone.

Perspective (noun): the capacity to view things in their true relations or relative importance

We did a lot of winning from 1979 to 1983 when I was at IU. Winning mattered. It sold a lot of tickets. It attracted a lot of attention to the university. And it had the potential—as winning often does—of staining the fabric of the program.

It was my perspective then—and to this day—that the fabric of Indiana Basketball was the people. There's no question that the demands of the program were tough and to the point where I wondered if I was better off not being involved. I, and I am certain many others, carried on because of the people that were there with us.

Coach Knight had a way of bringing the best people inside the tent. The people associated with Indiana Basketball were quality men and women; persons of character, people who conducted themselves with integrity and genuine care about others. There weren't many knuckleheads.

I think about it all starting with Dave Skibinski and Pete Schroeder, who hired me as a manager. I'm grateful for the friendships formed with the likes of the managers, such as Mark Galenski; the players, especially Ted Kitchel; and, even the announcer, Chuck Crabb. I remember seeing Randy Wittman at church on Sunday mornings at 9 a.m. after we had just arrived home at 3 a.m. from a Saturday night road trip.

It just was an honor and privilege to be part of it all. We represented Indiana University and Hoosier Basketball. Yes, we won games and championships, but we won so much more because our perspective of the program was rooted in the quality people that comprised it.

Today, I'm fortunate to live (in Columbus, Ohio) within driving distance to Bloomington. My perspective to the program is the farthest it has ever been. Yet, my perspective of the program hasn't changed. The four years I attended Indiana University and worked for Coach Knight as part of the men's basketball program were perhaps the best four consecutive years of my life. The lessons I learned and the people I met went a long way toward shaping the person I am today. My perspective? I'm grateful, thankful, and very blessed to have been part of it all.

Joe "Joe B." Black, M.S.

Athletic Director, Perry Meridian Middle School
Indianapolis, Indiana

IU Manager: 1978-1983

Degrees Earned: B.S., Social Studies Education, Indiana University, 1983,
M.S., Education and Principals License, 1988
Administrative License, Indiana University, 2000

Joe Black has spent thirty years in education. He was a US History and Government teacher at Perry Meridian High School for eight years, as well as Head Basketball Coach at Perry Meridian for three years. He began his career in administration as Dean of Boys at Southport High School in Indianapolis before becoming Athletic Director at Perry Meridian Middle School in 2001. He is in his twelfth year in that position.

Telling Stories Never Gets Old

My first exposure to Coach Knight was in the Fall of 1977. I would accompany my high school coach to Bloomington to watch practices occasionally. Coach Hoover knew I wanted to coach and teach someday, and there was no better way to learn than to watch an IU practice.

I was and am still amazed about the efficiency of an IU Basketball practice under Coach Knight. There was never a second wasted and I truly attempted to instill that in the teams I coached over the years. The planning, effort and foresight that was put into every practice was amazing. The basketball court was his classroom.

Preparation for games was exactly the same way. There was never a stone left unturned and if there was something to know about an opponent, our players would know it. They would have had to add in new plays prior to the Indiana game for our team to be fooled.

I don't know if it was just the way I am or if I was incredibly influenced by Coach Knight, but our relationships with players were similar. He cared deeply for his players but from the outside looking in, it may not have seemed that way. Those who were part of the day to day operations of the program knew it. We have all heard stories of the tremendous display of kindness to those who have been in his program, long after their playing days were over. It is Coach Knight's way of paying you back for the time and effort you put into the program. For example, my parents were able to see some games, especially the Final Four in Philadelphia in 1981, due to his generosity. They never forgot about that, and I will never forget as well.

I have so many examples of little things that he did for me, that he will probably never remember, but I sure will. In 1982, we lost to Alabama Birmingham in the NCAA Tournament in Nashville, Tennessee. Gary Sims and I were the two Senior Managers that year and he wanted to make sure we flew home with the team one final time since our "eligibility" was over. I will never be able to sufficiently thank Coach Knight for his thoughtfulness as it meant so much to me.

Coach Knight genuinely respected his elders in the coaching profession, especially notable coaches such as Pete Newell, Fred Taylor, Claire Bee, etc. I believe this was a big influence on me in my coaching career. I often thought to myself, "If Coach Knight can seek out advice from people about the game, I sure can." Those that I later worked for such as Steve Witty, Bill Springer and Ed Siegel, all in the Indiana Basketball Hall of Fame, were highly influential in molding my basketball philosophy.

Finally, when you get a firsthand view every day of a basketball genius and innovator at work, someone known worldwide for his creation of motion offense, the person coaches from all over the world would visit with in Bloomington for weeks at a time to listen to and learn from, how could I not have been influenced in my basketball coaching career by Coach Knight? The game is different today, but in some ways it is the same. The "little things" are the difference between winning and losing most of the time. Coach Knight instilled those little things in his players. He instilled them in me personally. I am a better coach, better teacher, and better administrator for having worked under Coach Knight.

Chuck Fattore

President, Logistics, RR Donnelley & Sons
Bolingbrook, IL
Basketball Manager: 1979-1983
Graduate Assistant IU: 1983-1984
Degree Earned: B.A. Telecommunications, Indiana University, 1983

Charles E. Fattore is President of RR Donnelley Logistics Services a $1.3 billion premier third party provider of logistics management solutions. Prior to joining DLS, Chuck spent ten years managing distribution and transportation operations for Bank One and its predecessor company, First Chicago NBD. He is also Chairman of the National Postal Policy Council and serves on the Board of Directors of Postcom. He is past chairman of the American Bankers Association Postal Committee and served on the Executive Board of the Mailers Technical Advisory Committee (MTAC); he was also on the Postmaster General's Competitive Services Task Force. Earlier in his career Chuck spent five years as an assistant to Bob Knight and the Indiana University Basketball program (four as a manager and one as a graduate assistant coach) and was also an assistant coach at the University of Colorado in Boulder. He currently serves as President of the Neuqua Valley High School Hockey Club and Co-Chair of the Amateur Hockey Association of Illinois' High School Committee. Chuck and his wife Nancy have two sons, Andrew and Christopher, and reside in Naperville IL.

The Side No One Sees ... Lessons Learned

Of all the amazing things that I witnessed during my time working for Coach Knight at Indiana, I am really surprised that one conversation stands out among all others. Maybe it was because it was an example to me of how so many people or critics of Coach Knight never really knew him and never had the great opportunity that I was afforded to see him work each and every day for over five years. The story takes place at Assembly Hall and Coach Knight's youngest son Pat must have been in 7th or 8th grade. On a fairly regular basis, Pat used to come over to the Indiana Basketball practices and watch and shoot around. This day when he arrived at practice, Coach Knight called him over; Coach was crouched at one end of the court under the basket where drills were taking place. When Pat made his way over, Coach Knight looked at him and asked, "Did you do anything today to help anyone?" When Pat hesitated before answering, Coach Knight said to him, "You have a lot of things that other people don't, you should make sure you do something each and every day to help someone."

When people ask me (which happens nearly every day) what it was like to work for Coach Knight, I tell them that they and the media really have no idea what Coach Knight is like, because he only lets them see what he wants them to. This story stuck with me and is something I have tried to use with my own children. In this story, Coach Knight wasn't the Head Coach at Indiana, he wasn't the Head Coach of the USA Olympic Basketball team, and he wasn't maybe the greatest college basketball coach in history. He was simply a father teaching his young son a lesson and trying to instill certain values in him. It is a story that I am sure made a lasting impression on Pat, as well as one basketball manager that happened to be standing close enough to overhear the conversation. It is the type of story that very few outside the Indiana Basketball program ever got to see.

When I look back on my time at Indiana University, I am struck by the fact that by the time I left to go coach at the University of Colorado, I really felt like I had learned more that would help me in life from working for Coach Knight and basketball program than I did in the classrooms of a very fine university. There were lessons learned that have been helpful in both my professional and personal life and that I still use today. If I were to pick one that has been most helpful, it would be the lesson about improvement. While at Indiana, I had the good fortune of not only being a manager but also spending more than a year as a graduate assistant coach. This gave me the opportunity to be involved in coaches' meetings and spend time in the coaches' locker room (aka "the dungeon") nestled in the corner of Assembly Hall opposite the players' locker room watching endless film. One of the things that Coach Knight asked us on a fairly regular basis was, "Are we any better today than we were yesterday?" Coach would tell us there are only three things that can happen each day, "We get better, we stay the same, or we get worse and two of those are bad." He was obsessed with our improving as a basketball team. I have been able to take that same approach to running a business and ask my leadership team that same question. It tends to keep us very focused and working on those things that we may not be particularly good at. This is a simple notion but very powerful.

One of the other things that made a huge impression on me and I suspect that most will find surprising is how Coach Knight solicited input from everyone before making decisions. Many people have the impression that Coach is very dictatorial and while it is true that there is no question who is making the final decision, people may be surprised to know how much he solicits input from others. Obviously there were those he respected both in and out of basketball that he reached out to on a regular basis. People like the great Pete Newell, his good friend John Havlicek, Red Auerbach, Tony LaRussa, etc. (talk about an education, just getting to meet those folks and listen to them and Coach Knight tell stories at dinner was incredible!)

But Coach Knight also sought input from others, particularly his assistant coaches. One of the best illustrations of this occurred with the 1983-84 team. We were playing in the East Regional at the Omni in Atlanta and our first game was against North Carolina and Michael Jordan. After we had finished our morning shoot around, we came back to the hotel and the coaches met in Coach Knight's suite to finalize the game plan for that evening. Our line-up that year had been somewhat unsettled with many different players starting games. Coach Knight went around the room to each assistant coach and asked us who we thought should start and how we thought that line-up should match up, in other words who would guard whom? Obviously the match up problem was Jordan, you put a bigger player on him and he steps outside and shoots jump shots, a smaller player and he takes him down low and posts him up, neither a great option. We each gave Coach Knight our thoughts on the line-up and he probed with each of us why we thought our line-up made the most sense. At the end of the discussion, after taking everything in, Coach looks at us and gave us the his decision and then in a moment that will live in Indiana Basketball history, he said, "And we'll put Dakich on Jordan and have him play underneath him, we'll give him the jump shot, but we have to take away his ability to go to the rim at all costs."

Interesting story, but for me it was a great example of wanting those around you to give you the best information they have and their best thoughts, and you take that and try and make the best decision. Coach Knight honestly wanted to know what we all thought and then with that information he made the decision, which was clearly the correct one. He may have known all along what he wanted to do but that did not stop him from asking our opinion. I have tried to do the same thing in my business career. I do not want a bunch of "yes" people around me. I want everyone's best thinking and, given that, I am confident that I will make the right decision. An invaluable lesson I learned from Coach Knight.

The lessons were many and I believe they have all helped me in some way as I have gone through life. Preparation, loyalty, motivation, the constant striving for excellence all lessons learned from Coach Knight and IU Basketball. Has there been a better coach in sport at any time? Probably not. Has there been a better teacher anywhere? Definitely not.

Jerome Davis, Jr.
Math Teacher, Hamilton Southeastern High School
Fishers, IN
IU Manager: 1981-1984
Degrees Earned: B.S., Education, Indiana University, 1984
M.S., Secondary School Administration, Indiana University, 1996

Jerry Davis has worked his way up in the high school coaching ranks since leaving Indiana University. He has coached at Pampa and South Garland High Schools in Texas as well as Marion, Hamilton Southeastern, Triton Central and Wawasee High Schools in Indiana. He was the head coach of the latter two. In his 21 years of coaching basketball, he has coached 49 players who have gone on to play college basketball. He has been named to "Who's Who Among American Teachers" on three occasions. He is the proud father of two children, Brice and Bailey.

The Bus Lesson
We had beaten Richmond in the opening round of the 1984 NCAA Tournament the weekend before, and it was the first Saturday game we had won in a month. I can remember Coach coming into the locker room before

practice on Sunday, extremely positive and confident with this team that had fizzled at the end of the season.

We had lost three of our last six regular season games and what should have been a share of the Big Ten title. The team had lost eight games that year, all of them on Saturday. He simply told the team, "We're going to beat North Carolina and here is how we are going to do it …" This is not the way Coach typically prepares the team for an upcoming opponent. He tends to focus on the team's personnel and strengths and alerts them to things that must be taken care of or we are going to lose. He inspired confidence and lifted this cloud that had covered the team since losing to Miami of Ohio at home to start the season, and been amplified with losses to Kentucky, Purdue at home, and at Northwestern.

Everyone felt strongly that the winner of our game with Carolina would represent the East at the Final Four in Seattle. Virginia and Syracuse were playing in the other half of the bracket and we were certain we could get past either one of them. We had a great three days of practice and we definitely thought we were going to beat Carolina.

Even before we left for the trip, there had been much confusion about our travel plans and things were out of sync. Obviously if we lost to UNC, we would be home Thursday night and released to go home for spring break by Friday, Saturday at the latest. Coach had been named the Men's Olympic Coach for the coming summer. He had already been meeting with representatives of the Amateur Basketball Association of the United States of America (ABAUSA) about setting an agenda for the upcoming Olympic Trials and establishing a roster of players and coaches to be invited. Because we were headed into spring break and would not be missing classes, it made perfect sense to head on to Seattle. Coach Knight could work out the team and meet with the people at ABAUSA as needed. At Indiana, your spring break plans are to be playing in the tournament somewhere. We told the managers to pack for a week.

I was out of sync because Athletic Director Ralph Floyd was adamant about keeping everything the same as we had the previous week, down to using the same bus company and bus driver to haul us around Atlanta as we had used in Charlotte. It was the first Saturday game we had won in a month and the only meaningful Saturday win all year. Mr. Floyd meant well, but it turned into a total debacle.

Because the bus driver was from out of town, he needed a room and a place to park the bus, neither of which we had or would have had to worry about with a local bus service. Additionally, he did not know where to pick us up at the airport, the layout of the city with its one-way streets, or how to get us to the team entrance at the Omni Coliseum. Thus, getting to the arena from the airport took longer than expected. Once there, the driver headed down the wrong ramp and we could not make the turn at the end. We were running late for the press conference and scheduled shoot around. Coach stopped the bus and the team got out, jumped over some barriers, and banged on some doors just to get inside the arena.

My first "ass-chewing" of the week came shortly thereafter because the bus driver from a foreign city didn't know where he was going. I pointed out that I had advised against this earlier in the week. I was told to get it fixed—NOW! So, while the team was in their shoot around, I was with the bus driver learning the route from the arena back to the hotel and where the team should be delivered for tomorrow's game.

On Thursday, we upset Michael Jordan and the University of North Carolina. The legend of Michael Jordan was in its infancy but he was still Player of the Year and had a lot to do with them being ranked #1 in the country. They also started All-American Sam Perkins and future pros Kenny Smith and Brad Daugherty. Danny Dakich stopped Jordan, we won the game, and Dakich is forever an Indiana legend. I can remember Coach's words after the game, "Boys, you get me to Seattle and I'll figure out a way to win the damn thing!"

In the Regional Final, we played Virginia, the 5th place team out of the ACC (Atlantic Coast Conference). At game time, the decision still had not been made on whether we would go on to Seattle from Atlanta or if we would return to Bloomington. Worst case scenario was we would spend the night in Atlanta and fly out in the morning. Losing was never a part of the discussion—but we did, 50-48.

On the return trip from Atlanta, I was booted from the plane at the last minute. Coach needed my seat to take back a member of ABAUSA with him to Bloomington to talk about the Olympic Trials. I had ridden with the team all year long. My main travel responsibility as a Senior Manager was logistics: getting the team to the airport from Assembly Hall, to the hotel, arena and back again. Also, getting players up in the morning, to meals, meetings as well as assisting with ticket assignments, screening calls and filling out expense reports.

I was sick to my stomach over the loss, the only time I had been that way my entire life. I was cramped in the back seat of Coach Jim Crews's car staring out the window, dreading the eight hour car ride and drowning in my own thoughts of being a part of IU Basketball and out of nowhere—it hit me. I felt like I was in a free fall without a parachute ... DAMN!!!! I had not ordered the bus to meet the team back in Bloomington. What in the world am I going to do? Coach is going to be so angry!!

We pulled over at the next exit and I frantically tried to reach someone at the bus barn. I exhausted my calling card trying to get in touch with the people in Bloomington. It was Saturday evening, the campus had shut down for spring break and most of the athletic department—anyone who could help bail me out of this situation was like us, returning from Atlanta. I was frantic and called every number in my book. There had not been a problem with the bus since my freshman year and I had made it through this year with everything going perfect—except this last bus ride. I finally got in touch with someone and they said they would try to get in touch with a driver and get someone out there as soon as they could. Needless to say, I felt like crap all the way home but now for another reason. As it turned out, the plane arrived in Bloomington two hours before the bus did. Thankfully the weather was nice enough in Bloomington as the team spent those two hours on the tarmac before getting back to Assembly Hall.

I got back to Assembly Hall about 2:30 a.m. and went to the locker room to see what needed to be done. There was a bit of clean up and a note on the white board, "Jerry—where was the _____ bus??? See me Monday." I was devastated and my fellow managers' reaction was anything from all out laughter to shaking their head and saying, "I'm glad it's not me!" It was such a bonehead move and totally inexcusable. I should have ordered the bus as a back-up plan. That was always the way we did things, get them done first, worry about expenses later.

I spent all day Sunday stewing about this and could not get rid of the knot in my gut. I even went by the office twice on Sunday to see if anyone was in the office. I needed to talk to Coach but I didn't want to talk to Coach. No one was there either time. I know I didn't sleep more than a couple of hours that night but was at the office at 8:30 a.m. MaryAnn Davis, Coach's secretary, had not been there very long when I arrived and I sat there waiting until about 11 a.m. when Coach finally arrived. He didn't even acknowledge me when he arrived but talked with MaryAnn about some things, handed her a stack of mail he had read with notes of response, and then asked her to get a couple of people on the phone for him. He then called me in the office and ripped me pretty good. He began recapping the bus screw-ups for the weekend, not leaving one thing out, capped off by having to sit for two hours waiting on a bus and how the team had to stand outside. I became more paralyzed the longer he went. I just stood there and listened. At the end of his spiel, he told me to turn in my keys and not to show up at the banquet, that I was done and he didn't want me around anymore. It was all I could do to hold it together.

I had previously decided that if we got beat by Carolina, I would stay in Bloomington and use the time over break to catch up on my classes. The campus was dead, my roommate was gone, the players were gone, there was no one to talk to. I just kept playing Coach's comments over and over in my mind—dying a little more every time. I couldn't figure out how I was going to tell my mom and dad not to come to the banquet because I wouldn't be there. I did not get a lot accomplished with the books—I slept a lot as I was emotionally exhausted. On Wednesday, I got a call from MaryAnn and she told me Coach needed to see me and he was leaving town in an hour. I wasn't sure what else I had done that he would need to see me about, maybe he was pulling the partial scholarship I had received my senior year. I played things over in my mind about how I was going to apologize hoping he would let me come to the banquet.

When I got there, MaryAnn buzzed him to let him know I was waiting. He called for me to come in to his office almost immediately. From her desk to his office were some of the longest and most timid steps I have ever taken. As soon as I appeared in the doorway, he started talking to me like Saturday and Monday had never happened—this in and of itself, threw me for a loop. He told me the Olympic Trials would be here April 17-22 and he would be bringing in 70 or more players and 50 or more coaches from around the country. ABAUSA would send me itineraries and I would need to make arrangements to have them picked up and shuttled back to Bloomington. They would be assigned rooms and the players would need to be shuttled to the field house three times a day for practice and to the Student Union for meals. The coaches would need transportation and they could get themselves around. He wanted to know if I could get that done.

Without thinking I told him, "Yes."

He told me to call the transportation department and car dealers and tell them what I needed for the trials. He said, "Ok" and I knew we were done.

I turned and walked out and got as far as MaryAnn and I turned around and stood in his doorway again, "I will need some keys to get started."

"See MaryAnn"

I figured what the hell, "...and the banquet?" And he just raised his chin as if to say don't make me answer that—and I smiled, "Got it"

After getting my keys and heading down the ramp from the office – I realized he had just done to me what I had seen him do 100 times before to the players. He had challenged me. I remember telling myself, "I will not screw this up!" I didn't.

Since my freshman year at IU, people who knew I was part of the program would want to discuss the latest news on Indiana Basketball. Coach was frequently in the news for a comment he had made in the newspaper or on his weekly TV show. I studied him closely as I had decided to be a basketball coach since my sophomore year of high school. What people never understood was how great a teacher he was. People wanted the scoop or to get the lowdown on what they thought was going on behind the black curtain that sealed off the view to his classroom. My point to them was always the same; you have to see him teach, he didn't just raise hell with them because they made a mistake. He shows film, he walks players through situations; he explains clearly and then sets up drills to teach the player how to react in a game—he goes over it until the player gets it and then he reviews it again. When the player does not perform, he is frustrated. But the part that no one recognizes or sees is the progress a player makes, or how they continue to improve first mentally and then physically. Least of all, they don't understand why. They just know that they are all very good players by the time they leave Indiana.

Everyone in the program was challenged daily by Coach Knight and as a result, assistant coaches become head coaches, players and managers become successful in their chosen field and are good fathers. What people never see is the way Coach challenges them. Unless you are there, unless you are part of it you don't understand the challenge. Do not confuse the tongue lashing you see Coach give a player as the challenge—it's the consequence. When someone invests time into you, holds you accountable and doesn't toss you to the side because you have failed—it is because they believe in you and that you are capable of more than you are showing. The challenge, where everyone gets better, is the "next time."

Coach is a masterful teacher to players but it carries over to his coaches and the managers. His expectation for you in all areas is greater than anything you think you can achieve and he uses your errors to make you better. He expects you to handle the job in front of you and when you don't, he is going to let you know about it. Most important—he *never* forgets. It's because he never forgets and is always challenging that people around him achieve high levels of success in whatever they do after leaving IU Basketball.

As a leader of young people, it's easy to say, "He can't do it. Let's get someone else who can," or to change what it is you are trying to do. When you mess up, he is going to get on you; it's a badge of honor, his way of telling you he thinks you are better than that. What he is masterful at is he will let things ride. He makes you reflect on your mistakes and then finds something to personally challenge you. Almost always, it is something more difficult than what you have already screwed up and been reprimanded for. What comes from within you is a strong determination to not let yourself, him or the program down. You remember his being upset with you and how his words cut you last time and you take on that challenge, saying to yourself almost with a vengeance—"Watch me, I will show you"—"I will show you I can do this!!"—and you do. Now you have grown and matured and you *ARE* better than that.

That screw up with the bus is something that I still take seriously today. I have been able to apply it in my coaching and used it as a cornerstone for the way I go about coaching kids. I am not perfect but a lot of coaches cater to the good kids and yell at the not-so-good ones. I have always tried to hold *all* my kids accountable, because it gives them value, expectations, unites them, and makes each of them part of a common cause. Kids will succeed in whatever parameters you build for them as long as you teach and invest time in them, are consistent, fair and let them know you believe in them. Too many young people who have achieved success on the court or in the classroom early in life become average. For some reason, an elevated level of success makes it so adults as well as peers no longer hold them accountable. Instead, they provide allowances that end up crippling them. As a leader of young people on the court and in the classroom, I try to believe in all of them, point out their shortcomings, and make sure they know I still believe in them. I have never given preferential treatment to the kid who was an "A" student or the star of my team. I have tried hard to treat them all the same, but differently. Everyone has expectations, everyone has consequences, and they always feel challenged to become more than they themselves believe they can be.

I learned this from Coach Knight.

Joseph P. Gleissner

Product Team Lead, RR Donnelley
Crawfordsville, IN
IU Manager: 1980-1984
Degree Earned: B.S., Management and Organizations, Kelley
School of Business, Indiana University, 1984

Joe Gleissner is a Product Team Lead in Customer Service for RR Donnelley in Crawsfordsville, Indiana. RR Donnelley is a world leader in print and digital services. The Crawfordsville Division is a Bible, book and directory print and bind facility. Joe has worked in Crawfordsville for 24 years.

Joe is married to Ann Gleissner. They have three children: Kristina, Jennifer and Andrew. They live in Brownsburg, Indiana.

Honor in Service, Getting the Job Done

As many know, growing up in Indiana, Hoosiers have a simple work ethic of getting the job done. Many value that the result is the recognition we all strive for. We aren't flashy, we aren't show men or women; we let our results speak for who we are and what we accomplish.

In my years with Indiana Basketball, I learned that early. Coach Knight demanded that we all put in the effort that would earn the expected results.

I grew up in Mishawaka, Indiana, in the 1960's and 70's. Mishawaka is located between South Bend and Elkhart in the shadow of Notre Dame's Golden Dome. Like most boys, I grew up loving sports, and being a Hoosier, basketball was the highest on my list. I played for Marvin Wood at Mishawaka. Coach Wood gained fame as the coach of the Milan Indians in the 1954 Indiana State Championship. Most know that story inspired the great movie, *Hoosiers*. Coach Wood and Coach Knight showed many of the characteristics that were displayed by Coach Dale in the movie. The writer of *Hoosiers*, Angelo Pizzo, is a Bloomington native and a huge Indiana fan so you can see how some of Coach Dale's character was scripted.

Coach Wood was a very inspirational person, both on and off the court. His guidance helped me get an interview to become a manager at Indiana.

The start of my career as an Indiana manager was the direct result, of all things, Purdue playing in the NCAA Final Four in 1980. Due to the Final Four being in Indianapolis that year, the Indiana High School State championship was delayed a week so the Semi-state portion (equivalent to the NCAA Regionals) was held the same weekend. Mishawaka had already lost in the always tough South Bend Sectional, my senior year. Coach Wood, several coaches, and players attended the Fort Wayne Semi-state as fans. During the break between games, we listened to Purdue playing UCLA in Indianapolis. It happened that one of the Mishawaka team managers from our 1979 team was a freshman manager for Purdue's team. While we listened, Coach Wood asked about me wanting to be a manager at IU. He contacted Coach Knight to see what I needed to do, then set up the interview for when I arrived in August, 1980.

I met with Coach Jim Crews and Senior Managers Steve Skoronski and Gary Sims. I knew immediately that this opportunity would be one that very few could or would be offered. I accepted the offer and immediately shaved my first moustache as required to be in the program.

The environment under Coach Knight and his staff was do what is expected and get the job done. The managerial hierarchy was definitely military style. You earned your "stripes" as you go. Freshmen were expected to be on the court, dressed and ready for practice. We participated in drills, rebounding, setting screens, defense, officiating, recording stats, filming, etc., whatever was needed to prepare the team to be ready in the Big Ten and NCAA.

The Fall of 1980 brought great expectations. Indiana was to be a top team with Isiah Thomas coming back for his sophomore year, Ray Tolbert, Randy Wittman, Ted Kitchel, Landon Turner, Glen Grunwald, Phil Isenbarger, Jim Thomas, Tony Brown, Steve Risley, and more back from a very successful season in 1979-80. I knew the program and the team were big but never expected the pressure that was present from the start. This was the big time.

Coach Knight's practices were always well prepared. We started at a certain time and went as long as he wanted, or on some days, could stand. I recall the first day. He and Isiah were speaking at the end of the court. I was dressed and on the court. All seemed well. Coach and Isiah ended their conversation. Isiah was smiling as he typically did. About twenty to thirty minutes into practice. Isiah had several turnovers and made some poor choices. Coach corrected a few things and play resumed. It happened again. Again, more coaching and feedback, then more poor play. Coach kicked Isiah out of practice. A shock to all.

I was closest to the locker door so I was the manager to unlock the door to let Isiah in. He was not pleased. He was upset and confused. I waited in an area of the locker room that couldn't be seen from the door or the locker area. My first day. I didn't know what to do. I stayed there until I heard the door fly open and Coach enter. He promptly ordered me to get out of the locker room with a booming command in Coach Knight's choice of words. Visibly shaken, I complied. I listened to Coach and Isiah review the day's practice with elevated voices and some choice language. Coach then left the locker room and walked past me with his head down. He glanced my way to say a quick "sorry about that." I then learned that Coach was setting a tone with this team. He had intentionally kicked out the star of the team. They learned that nobody was going to be above the others. All were accountable and would need to follow his direction.

That experience has been very influential. I think about it often and it makes a great story. Coach Knight had sent a message to the team and staff but I am sure most didn't know that he had intended to do that. I saw a different side to his actions. He had seen that the action had left me looking confused and intimidated in the hall but he calmed my nerves with a quick, assuring apology. Over time, we managers would joke or try to predict what Coach would do. Sometimes, he would take a successful team and put them in their place by kicking them out of practice. He would take a struggling team and give them a break by no extra practice or film time. He placed all on edge. I learned that your recent performance didn't always predict your future performance. You have to perform your best at all times or there would be consequences that you can't control. Coach Knight was scripting the team's physical and mental performance. For more than 70 percent of his games and three NCAA Championships, he got it right.

From that point, I was less intimidated by him and respected that he was very observant to all that was happening. He influenced me greatly in that he was willing to do what was needed to gain the expected result. We learned quickly that the expectation was to do what was needed. The reward was the honor that the job was done successfully.

Greg Ryan, D.D.S.
Dentist, Fishers Family Dentistry
Fishers, Indiana
IU Manager: 1982-1985
Degrees Earned: B.S., Education, Indiana University, 1985
M.S., Education, University of South Alabama, 1987
D.D.S., Indiana University School of Dentistry, 1996

Upon graduating from IU in 1985 Greg worked one year as a teacher and coach at Tipton, Indiana High School. He then served a year as a Graduate Assistant Coach at the University of South Alabama while earning his master's degree. His next five years were spent as a teacher at Hamilton Southeastern Schools. Next he decided to follow in his father's footsteps and applied to dental school. Greg is currently in private practice in Fishers, Indiana. He and his wife, Diane, have two sons who are both IU students.

Teamwork and Resourcefulness
I am so fortunate to have had the opportunity to work as a student manager for Coach Knight. I have always viewed it as the next best thing to having been a player for him. I need to thank a fellow manager, Joe Gleissner, for recommending that I apply for the position. Without his encouragement I would have missed out on one of the great experiences in my life. The lessons that I learned about life and basketball are innumerable.

Coach Knight's definition of discipline has always stood out to me:
1. Doing what you have to do.
2. Doing it when you have to do it.

3. Doing it the best that you possibly can.

4. And doing it that way every time.

Clearly, that definition applies to anything in life.

Coaching phrases such as "Don't shoot as an afterthought," "Move with a purpose," and "Make your dribble take you somewhere" are all quotes that I used when coaching the teams of my own sons. When talking about players, Coach would say that all of them can look, but very few could actually *SEE*. He also frequently said that players can hear, but few *LISTEN*. These thoughts are etched in my mind and hopefully some of the kids with whom I worked.

Being a student manager required some travel for road games. Many times the phone in our hotel rooms would ring and it would be Coach Knight with a "special request." While in New York City he asked us to go out and get him some pistachio nuts. Another time in Columbus, Ohio he said that he wanted a milkshake. But it needed to be authentic, not from some machine. Obviously, these were things that he wanted. But we often wondered if, in his own way, he was just challenging us to see if we could deliver on his specific requests!

Along these lines, the story that I would like to share occurred in the summer of 1984. This was an exciting time because the Olympic basketball team was practicing in Bloomington. What a thrill it was to walk into the locker room and see players such as Michael Jordan, Patrick Ewing, and Chris Mullin (as well as a guy named Steve Alford)!

In preparation for the Summer Games in Los Angeles, an exhibition game against some NBA All Stars had been scheduled in the newly constructed Hoosier Dome. We all took the bus up to the game and unloaded our gear in the locker room. Shortly after, Coach Knight summoned me to a room down the hall where he and a few of his cronies had settled. He stated that he wanted some hamburgers, but *NOT* from a fast food place (Coach always treated his friends and confidantes to the best). Well, being only 22 and not very familiar with downtown Indianapolis, I found myself in a very challenging predicament!

So, as was often the case, I sought out team trainer Tim Garl for advice.

He introduced me to a man named Mark Miles, who was a member of the prestigious Columbia Club. He agreed to order the food and have it put on his tab. But the question of how I was going to get over there and back remained. Mark put me in contact with Richard Blankenbaker; at that time he was the Director of Public Safety for the city of Indianapolis. He arranged for a police jeep to drive me over to the Indianapolis Circle, wait, and then transport me back to the Dome. While in the Columbia Club a staff member made a comment to the effect of "We are not typically involved in the carry-out business!"

When I returned to Coach Knight with the hamburgers on china plates with tin covers he seemed to be quite impressed! I was relieved that my mission had been a success. But I could not have accomplished it without teamwork and some resourcefulness.

Thank you, Coach Knight, for allowing me to play a small part in Indiana Basketball. So now when watching a game with my sons and one of them says, "Don't shoot as an afterthought" please know that your legacy has been passed on to the next generation!

Jim Kelly, M.S.

Dean of Students, Cary-Grove High School
Cary, Illinois
Adjunct Professor, Aurora University
Aurora, Illinois

IU Manager: 1982-1986

Degrees Earned: B.S., Business Marketing, Indiana University, 1986
M.S., Curriculum and Instruction, North Central
College, 1999, M.S., Administration, Northeastern
Illinois University, 2001

Jim Kelly is a Dean of Students at Cary-Grove High School and an Adjunct Professor at Aurora University. He has been married to Catherine for 22 years and is the proud father of Claire, Patrick and Jack. After leaving IU, Kelly worked for Airborne Express and American Airlines in Sales and Marketing. Jim earned a teaching degree and began instructing economics and history at Crystal Lake South High School in 1994. He became a Dean at Cary-Grove High School in 1997. He is a past president of the Illinois Dean Association, Fox Valley Dean Association, Illinois Dean of the Year in 2009, current president of the Cary-Grove Crimestoppers, a member of Rotary, member of the Irish American Heritage Center in Chicago, sponsors the high school's community service club Interact, and he is a dual Irish/American Citizen.

Lessons of a Lifetime

Failing to make the Indiana University baseball team was one of the best things that ever happened to me. That disappointment led me to the Hoosier Basketball program. Even though I did not play varsity basketball in high school, I was intrigued by the success, integrity and high quality of people associated with IU Basketball. If I could get involved in the basketball program, I thought that I could learn the intangibles that would help me become a successful person. I decided to interview for a basketball manager position and became part of the IU Basketball family in the fall of 1982.

During my four years at IU, I learned valuable lessons and gained experiences that help me everyday. As a dean of students at a high school, my job is very hectic and I make hundreds of difficult decisions each day. I deal with school-crisis situations, angry students, and unhappy parents. The ability to prioritize, analyze, make tough decisions and keep calm in pressure situations are skills I learned while I was part of the IU Basketball program. Coach Knight gave me the opportunity to be a leader. IU Basketball is where I learned to solve problems, overcome difficult situations, prioritize, maintain a positive attitude, take responsibility, stand up for what is right, deal with pressure, deal with adversity, and give back to people in need. I not only use these skills, but I am able to share them with the young adults I work with on a daily basis.

When asked about my experiences with Coach Knight, most people expect me to tell them about a verbal outburst, a tirade he was involved in, or how he mistreated someone. Instead, I tell them about the times he visited kids in hospitals, how he would give back speaking fees at fundraisers, when he would pick the perfect time to compliment someone or how he took the time to honor people who had done great things. Always doing the right thing was something that was (and still is) important to Coach. He instilled this value in me and all those who went through the IU Basketball program.

In part, Coach's philanthropy gave me the insight to work with students and start a community service club at my school. Through this group, I have led teenagers and instilled the importance of giving back to our community. In the past ten years, this group (Cary-Grove Interact) has raised hundreds of thousands of dollars for charity and has volunteered thousands of hours to help people in need. I attribute my desire to work with and contribute to others directly to the lessons that Coach Knight taught me.

There are many favorite memories I have during my time at IU. One of the times that will always stand out is the week we were getting ready to play North Carolina in the Sweet Sixteen of the 1984 NCAA Tournament. The Tar Heels were much more talented and the experts thought we would lose by double digits. Michael Jordan, Sam Perkins and a host of future NBA stars were on that team. I specifically remember Coach beginning practice by confidently telling our team how we were going to beat North Carolina. He instilled confidence in the team and described the game plan which would allow us to accomplish that goal. After hearing Coach's comments, I believed that I could put on an IU jersey and hold Michael Jordan to ten points. If you are an IU fan, you probably remember that distinction went to Dan Dakich. The Hoosiers went on to defeat the Tar Heels by a 72-68 margin and one of the biggest upsets in college basketball history. The speech and experience stuck with me. I truly believe that my "can do" and positive attitude come directly from my experiences with the IU Basketball program.

I have been the disciplinarian at Cary-Grove High School for the last fourteen years. I attribute my ability to do my job well to my background and the experiences I had growing up. Every day I use skills I learned from the IU Basketball program. All of those who worked for coach knew that he demanded we do the right thing all of the time. While he coached, he stood for more than just wins and losses. A large part of his formula for success included working hard, working smart, working together, being efficient, and doing everything the right way. Go figure, just like Coach Knight, I am a disciplinarian and I love it.

Coach, thanks for all that you have done for me and the thousands of others you have influenced in a very positive way.

Michael J. McGlothlin, ChFC, CLU, CFP®

Executive Vice President of Annuities, Ash Brokerage Corporation
Fort Wayne, IN
IU Manager: 1983-1987
Degree Earned: B.S., Business, Indiana University, 1987

Mike McGlothlin is the Senior Vice President, Annuities Division of Highland Capital Brokerage. His responsibilities include strategic direction, sales management, new account acquisition, and operations management for all annuity distribution within Highland Capital Brokerage. Mike also serves on the National Board of Directors for The Society of Financial Service Professionals and The Foundation for Financial Service Professionals. He is a 20-year veteran of the financial services industry having attained Million Dollar Roundtable status as a producer before becoming a corporate executive.

Real World Experience

During my freshman year at Indiana, Coach Knight served as the 1984 United States Men's Olympic coach. The Olympic Trials took place on campus with a full, one-week tryout culminating in two nights of exhibition game scrimmages. Over 70 of the top college players descended on Bloomington, IN to compete for spots on the team. Players such as Michael Jordan, Patrick Ewing, Charles Barkley, and John Stockton roamed the halls of Assembly Hall. Coach Knight assembled a team of the most respected basketball minds to work with him during the week to evaluate and select the team to represent the United States in the Los Angeles Olympics.

The basketball managers transported many of these athletes and coaches from the Indianapolis Airport south to Bloomington. As luck would have it, I had the privilege of picking up Coach Mike Krzyzewski ("Coach K"), one of Coach Knight's protégés and former players and assistant coaches. The drive from Indianapolis to Bloomington typically took 60 minutes. On my way to the airport, I was wondering how a freshman in college would hold up his end of the conversation during a one-on-one opportunity with one of the youngest, brightest coaches in America, not to mention a close friend of Coach Knight. The drive to Bloomington was one of the most memorable hours of my life and set the stage for multiple life lessons from Coach Knight. Coach K was genuinely interested in me as a person and a student. He asked questions about my first year on campus, how I prepared for classes, my social life, and my success in the classroom with all the hours spent in Assembly Hall as a basketball manager. We talked about how I was preparing for an upcoming test during the middle of the week of the trials.

What struck me most were his comments about taking advantages of the "real world experiences" that I had the opportunity to partake in the coming years as a manager. He said anyone could go to class, spend some time in the libraries, and hang out with friends while at college. But Coach Knight would place me in real world experiences, force me to balance time, prioritize activities, make difficult decisions, and expose me to people and experiences that others would only read about in business books. It would be those experiences that would make my four years at Indiana University more meaningful; however, it was my responsibility to take advantage of the opportunity and learn from the real world experiences that would be presented to me. The first came two days later when I ran into Coach K in the bowels of Assembly Hall. He had just been viewing hours and hours of videotape from the Soviet Union (they were still planning to come to the 1984 Olympics as of the time of the trials), Yugoslavia, and other European teams. As we approached each other, Coach K smiled and called me by name. I was impressed that he took the time to remember a freshman manager's name that he was unlikely to ever see again. After passing each other by about three or four steps, he stopped and turned around to ask me how I thought I did on the calculus test I had taken that morning at 8 a.m. – the one we talked about in the car several days prior. I walked away in awe that he remembered so much from our conversation and he took the time to ask in such granular detail. I'm confident that Coach K's willingness to take personal interest in other people began with Coach Knight.

Much like this short encounter, Coach Knight provided ample real world experiences that helped shape me and provide examples of leadership in the coming years as a student manager. The lessons learned remain with me today and have become a guidepost for me as I lead a corporate division. With the increased use of social media, email, and other technological advances I try to make people feel important much like Coach Knight did when someone visited practice. I have to be aware of my surroundings: my team's capabilities, the industry, and our strategic direction. I work in an industry that is ultra-competitive with commoditized products and services, and Coach Knight reinforced the need to prepare to win. And finally, I learned that in order to succeed, I benefit from the relationships, experiences, and support of those close to me and have worked in my industry before me.

It was not unusual to have a visitor or two at one of our practices at IU. Many times, Coach would invite a young coach to observe practice or a close friend would stop by to visit. Throughout the season, special guests would come to practice that made Coach Knight very happy to have the chance to visit with the team. Many of these individuals had visited Coach since he began coaching at Indiana. Some were elderly and were not as mobile. They sat near the entry to the basketball court just a few feet away from the coaches' locker room. Coach made sure that the players recognized the individual before the end of practice. While the players genuinely liked to be around basketball's legends, the joy that came over the person's face when the entire team came to shake his hand indicated that the visitor enjoyed the recognition and courtesy that these teenagers provided. Coach always stressed the impact that the players had on the brand and reputation of Indiana University. More important, he stressed the need to maintain a personal reputation that the university would be proud of as well. Reaching out to an elderly, long term supporter was simply expected—because it was the right thing to do and made that person feel special. Today, I take time to learn about my prospects, our top clients, our carriers, and my employees to make them feel part of the team and special. I remain intensely driven toward success, but I always try to take a step back and remain a real life person.

One of my favorite practices came during Christmas break my senior year. There were typically two-a-day practices when students were out of town on holiday breaks. The players went through their pre-practice paces—getting their ankles taped, stretching, and warm-up drills. Coach Knight appeared from his locker room with a good friend who had a popular fishing show on ESPN. Coach was carrying a fishing rod, and my thoughts immediately changed to "this is going to be an interesting practice." He introduced his guest and everyone shook hands. Coach then spent the next hour talking about fly fishing and how it relates to basketball and life. The teacher spoke about knowing your surroundings. When casting a fly rod, you have to pay attention to the current of the river, the depth of the water, and how the line might hit the water. You understand your limitations given your surroundings. Maybe the rocks you are standing on are too slippery due to a buildup of moss that prevents you from making a full cast. There might not be a good place to land your line due to a small margin of error caused by the surroundings. Coach talked about patience and adjusting your cast to where the fish were going to be versus dropping the line right on top of them. He stomped around the basketball court illustrating that you just can't slosh through the waters and still expect to have success fly fishing.

He translated these attributes to our current team. When one of our guards fed the low post, they could not expect one of our big men to catch the ball around his ankles at high speed. The ball needed to be delivered in a way that would help the big man pin his man and move to the basket. Likewise, we could not reasonably expect some of the bench players to shoot the basketball with the same accuracy as Steve Alford. We had to recognize who was on the floor and value their strengths. If someone was not good at shooting beyond the free throw line, don't throw him the ball 20 feet away from the basket expecting a score as the shot clock was winding down. It was about awareness, knowing your team, and knowing your opposition's weaknesses. I try to understand my team's strengths and weaknesses in the same manner. Our sales division is made up of a diverse group of employees that think, work, and process information unique from each other. It's my job to recognize each person's strength and try to put them in a position for maximum success. Coach is a master of getting the best out of his players—he did so because he put them in the best possible position for success.

If there is one phrase that I keep in the front of mind from my time at Indiana, it is "Everyone has a will to win; few have a will *to prepare to win."*

After losing to Cleveland State in the first round of the 1986 NCAA tournament, Coach Knight focused the team on execution. He constantly spoke about and used the Cleveland State game as an example of the importance of practicing for perfection, playing every possession, and executing a game plan. Every team had talented players. With the advent of cable and satellite television, great high school players were exposed to more college choices than ever before. Every team, including small mid majors, had enough talent to beat a perennial powerhouse like Indiana. We had to execute better than anyone else because we either had the same level of talent or even slightly less. Practices were designed to improve on our weaknesses as individuals and as a team; they included relentless repetition; and measuring success/failures at every practice.

In the financial services industry, every competitor has the exact same product due to regulation. I have to get my team "prepared to win." We have to be razor sharp in our client meetings to deliver unique and compelling solutions to our advisors and their clients. We have to understand the needs and objectives of all parties and deliver the expertise that moves the client forward using the products available to every one of our competitors. We simply have to be better than everyone else at the point of sale. That only happens at the sale (game time) when you have done it repeatedly in practice, learned about the industry needs and trends, and become a specialist in your field. How many times did Dick Vitale talk about "screen 45" when he talked about Brian Sloan setting the ultimate screens? Or, Steve Alford moving without the ball and being the best pure shooter.

Jim Rohn (business motivational speaker) says success happens overnight after years of repetition. Over the past three years, I have taken my fitness more seriously. I have completed four half marathons and two full marathons. There is no way that I would have completed any of those races without running the 90-100 miles each month leading up to the event. Everyone wants to win, but we need to make sure that we have the will to prepare to win – by doing all the non-glamorous activities prior to the win. Three years ago, I could only run 1 mile at a time. It takes preparation and building up to get where you ultimately want to be, but you can win your personal or professional championship by focusing on the preparation leading up to the win.

One lesson that has become more important to me lately is to surround myself and leverage the cumulative knowledge of my network. I can remember prior to big games taking messages to Coach Knight that a legendary coach such as Hank Iba, Pete Newell, or Bill Parcells was on the phone. Coach always reached out to successful people to learn information or techniques. I've come to realize that I don't have all the answers and the ones I do have aren't always the best. I regularly consult with a team of professionals that I value and can advise me on business or personal dilemmas. I regularly reach out to members of a highly respected network of trusted industry professionals through The Society of Financial Service Professionals; I consult with a business coach monthly; and gain direction from ownership on my division's progress. I welcome the quality input and try to take their teachings and improve my chances of success.

Coach Knight's real life experiences continue to be a strong compass for me today. His teachings of connecting to the real person and staying grounded are important for all leaders. Being aware of my surroundings and putting my division constantly in the best possible position for success can never be truer today with our difficult and changing economic environment. As I build a brand new division for my employer, I've been tested mentally and physically. I always reflect to make sure that I have prepared to compete in the market place. When I know that I have prepared fully, I become the calm and decisive leader that others look toward.

Scott Dolson

Assistant Athletics Director, Indiana University
Bloomington, IN
IU Manager: 1984-88
Degree Earned: B.S. Management, School of Public and Environment
Affairs, Indiana University, 1988

Scott Dolson is Deputy Director of Intercollegiate Athletics and oversees all external operations within the department. Previously he served as the Director of the Varsity Club for seven years. Dolson joined the Varsity Club staff in December of 1989 and worked in various roles including: major gifts, annual giving, volunteer network and the courtesy car program. In addition to his role as Deputy Director of Intercollegiate Athletics, Dolson has maintained his role as the fourth director of the Varsity Club and currently directs the athletic department's overall fund raising program for scholarships, annual giving, endowments, and athletic facilities. Following graduation from IU he worked for Tim Knight Enterprises. Dolson and his wife Heidi have five children, four boys and one girl.

Special Guests

There are lots and lots of unbelievable memories I have from the four years I spent as a basketball manager at Indiana University. In fact, the stories get better and better as the years go by!! I always enjoy seeing other former managers or players and swapping stories and laughs ... usually ending with a stomach ache from laughing so hard.

We all have a bevy of stories and lessons learned from our time around Coach Knight. The one memory I have on a serious side that I often think about when people ask me about Coach Knight is one that at least for me, sums up a lot about Coach Knight as a person.

We were at a typical practice in Assembly Hall over the Holiday break. The building was totally empty other than the coaches, players and managers. Practice was always closed except for a few invited guests but this day the building seemed particularly empty since the University and Assembly Hall were closed for the holidays. At one point I received word that a few managers needed to head over to the big garage door in the northeast corner of the Assembly Hall floor to let in a group that would be joining us that day to attend and watch practice. I did as directed and went over there with a couple of other managers.

When the bus arrived carrying the guests, it was clear that these guests were different from others that typically stopped by for a visit to practice. All of these guests were severely mentally and physically challenged. The majority of the people were in wheel chairs. In fact, one person was actually in some type of a mobility device that most resembled a bed. It was pretty tough to see the people who have to deal with such challenges every day ... I know it made all of us feel extremely fortunate. One by one the guests were all assembled along the north end of the basketball court and remained there for the last part of practice.

Once practice ended, I was at the end of the court situated close to our guests. I watched Coach Knight as he went down the line one by one and greeted each individual and talked to them. Some of the guests most likely did not even know who he was or where they were. Regardless of their individual challenge Coach Knight treated them all with enthusiastic respect and was able to get many of them to laugh, smile and connect in some way.

I vividly remember as he greeted the last guest thinking to myself that I would always remember that practice for many reasons. The obvious reasons to remember the practice were to always think of others, empathize for people who are facing tough challenges, and treat everyone with the same respect. The main reason I would never forget that practice was that Coach Knight made this special effort for these people without anyone else knowing but the players, managers and other coaches who were there that day. No media. No photographers. Nothing. He did it for the special guests to brighten their day and not for the positive publicity he could have gained from it. I learned by watching him that day that no matter what criticism might be hurled his way, this act of kindness was the way I would always remember Coach Knight.

I will always be grateful to Coach Knight for allowing me to be a part of the IU Basketball fraternity and for giving me the experience of a lifetime.

David Gottlieb
Business Owner, Ocean Printers, Inc.
Hollywood, Florida
IU Manager: 1984-1988
Degrees Earned: B.A., History, Indiana University, 1988

David Gottlieb is the owner of Ocean Printers in Hollywood, Florida. He has worked at the printing/copying/graphics design company since his graduation from Indiana University in 1988. Ocean Printers is a full service print and design shop. David married Ilene in 1998. They have two daughters, Jessica (12) and Rachel (9). David enjoys watching and attending college football and basketball games. David also enjoys going to the beach and vacations in Colorado. David and his family currently reside in Hollywood, Florida.

Second Generation
My experience with Coach Knight began long before I became a manager for the IU Basketball team. My father, Edward Gottlieb was a manager at Ohio State University while Coach Knight was a player for the Buckeyes in the late 1950's and early 1960's. They became very good friends and have maintained a friendship that has continued

through the years. Because of this friendship, I was given the opportunity to attend many IU games with my father, although I grew up in South Florida.

My father and I were huge IU and Coach Knight Fans! We traveled to Bloomington, as well as many other cities to see Coach Knight. I was able to attend many practices and meet the players and managers from many IU Basketball teams over the years. Since I was able to do this at such a young age and loving basketball as much as I did, becoming a manager gave me the opportunity to be around people and a program that I respected. I also knew that I was not going to be good enough or tall enough to play basketball, so becoming a basketball manager was an extremely significant experience in my life.

Managing the basketball team was not just about cleaning, getting water and hanging around a gym watching practices and games. It was so much more than that! I feel that being a manager for Indiana was like an internship for whatever career path that you chose. We were expected to learn all of the facets of running a practice, filming, keeping statistics, taking care of all the equipment and providing whatever else was needed for practices and games in Assembly Hall. The managers were a dedicated group of volunteers who loved the game of basketball and being a part of such a prestigious organization.

Being a manager gave me the opportunity to work with a great group of people and represent one of the greatest universities in this country. It was a great experience because it prepared us for the real world. Coach Knight was a great and significant influence in my life. I feel that he was, and still is a positive role model. He instilled a work ethic in us that is second to none. He also gave us a great will to win and succeed, not just on a basketball court, but in life. All his lessons were much more than just about the game of basketball, but about the game of life. He made team accomplishments much more important than individual accomplishments. It was all about working together and putting your individual statistics aside, so that the team could accomplish something greater. A perfect example happened in my junior year in 1987 when we won the NCAA Championship. We had a

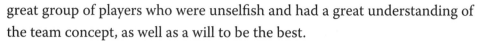

great group of players who were unselfish and had a great understanding of the team concept, as well as a will to be the best.

Being a part of the Indiana Basketball program, working for Coach Knight and working with all the other coaches and managers was an experience that I will cherish and never forget!

John E. Martin

Senior Territory Manager, Merck Animal Health
Martinsville, IN
IU Manager: 1986-1989
Degree Earned: B.S., Marketing, Indiana University, 1989

John Martin became a manager in the fall of 1986; he holds the unique position among the managers as he was a high school wrestler rather than being involved in basketball prior to attending IU. In addition to being a manager, he also worked part-time for Tim Knight in the World Famous General Store. John is a graduate of the Indiana University Kelley School of Business with a degree in marketing. Upon graduation, and with a recommendation from Coach Knight, he was hired into a sales position with Merck Animal Health, with whom he is still employed today as a senior territory manager. John lives in Martinsville, Indiana, with his wife Sherrie and four daughters.

Fuzz and Silence

Just prior to the NCAA tourney I remember thinking that I had survived my time with Indiana Basketball without feeling the full wrath of Coach Knight. We were in Tucson for the first round of the tourney and I was in charge of game films. The coaches had put together a series of shots of UTEP that they planned and they were to watch after the pregame meal at the hotel (that name escapes me but needless to say it was nice), I had set up the VCR and the TV just as I had a thousand times before. I was in a hurry, however, to get ready for pregame and the game. I, however, didn't realize that I had misconnected the patch cord from the VCR to the TV, thereby rendering it useless.

When Coach went to play the tape there was nothing but fuzz. He hit the button again assuming that it was the remote. Again fuzz and silence.

We jumped in to action to try and figure out what was wrong. Everyone was rushing around like chickens with our heads cut off. I kept looking at the hook up and it looked right. Then Coach Knight asked who set it up. I told him I did. He then asked me if it worked when I checked it. I looked at him and said ummmmm. That's when he went ballistic!!!! He yelled and rightfully so, he yelled at me!!!! He just went off! Then to make matters worse some program was going on in the ballroom next door to ours. A woman came down to our room opened the door and asked if we could keep it down. Coach then left the room. One of the other managers figured out what my error was and the team was able to watch the film. Afterward Joe Hillman came up to me and told me not to worry about it. Coach was going to go off on someone to get them ready for the game. I don't know if I have EVER prayed so hard for a victory.

After the game I was responsible to go back to the hotel and be there when the team got off the bus. Of course Coach was the first one off the bus. He looked at me and asked if the doors to the hotel worked. They were electric doors, the type that when you walk on the pad and they open automatically. I immediately turned ran over to the doors and tapped the pad with my foot. I then turned and said yes sir they work! He looked at me smacked me in the back of the head and said you won't #$&@ up like that again, will you? I said no sir! It has stuck with me to this day. Whenever I give a presentation I will check the equipment numerous times. Coach always has a way of expecting the best out of players and others around him. He demands it! My time with the program, and in particular Coach Knight, was more relevant to my business career than the time at Indiana University School of Business. Thanks for the opportunity to share this story!!!!

Nelson Nettles, J.D.

Lawyer and Partner, LeBlanc Nettles & Davis,
Brownsburg, Indiana

IU Manager: 1986-1989

Degrees Earned: B.A. Political Science, Indiana University, 1989
J.D., Law, Indiana University School of Law,
Bloomington, 1992

Nelson Nettles is a lawyer and a partner in the central Indiana law firm of LeBlanc Nettles & Davis. Prior to becoming a principal in that firm, he practiced at Norris Choplin Schroeder LLP, where he represented clients in civil litigation for 20 years. Nelson handles cases involving aviation, product liability, appellate practice, insurance coverage, subrogation, business disputes, federal court litigation, and employment law. Prior to joining Norris Choplin, Nelson clerked for Federal District Judge Larry J. McKinney and Magistrate Judge J. Patrick Endsley of the Southern District of Indiana. Nelson is admitted to practice before the United States Supreme Court, the Sixth and Seventh Circuit Courts of Appeal, and all Indiana state courts. Nelson and his wife Amy have 3 children, Alexander and identical twin girls Claire and Mia.

Basketball to Law

Beyond the Rim

Guys became student basketball managers at Indiana University for a variety of reasons. Many played basketball and wanted to continue the association with a sport they loved. Others became student managers because they had played high school ball with recruits or IU players. Some, I am sure, harbored dreams of being asked to step in and play for the team (for a few that dream came true). For many more, probably a majority of student managers, they hoped to go into coaching and wanted to learn from the best coach in the country in the Holy Land of basketball, which is Indiana. Still others joined perhaps to be associated with greatness, or to be associated with celebrities, as Indiana Basketball players are treated in Indiana and by Indiana Basketball fans. I think a few may have signed on just because they thought it was a cool thing to do during their years on campus - those people did not stay long when they discovered the work involved.

I did not seek a manager position for any of those reasons. I was not a basketball star in high school. Playing ball at the Franklin Boys Club and in elementary and middle school, after my freshman year in high school, I was done. I was not very good at basketball. I did not want to become a basketball coach, or any other kind of coach for that matter. I wanted to go to law school and become a lawyer. That was my driving goal.

Why would a person wanting to go to law school seek to spend an inordinate amount of his time with sports? The reason was quite simple. Indiana Basketball and Coach Knight represented to me the best of their field. I wanted to be with those who strived to be their best. I believed that as you associate yourself with those who work hard, you will work hard to do your best. Some kinds of peer pressure are good. These seemed to be good peers to have. Certainly better than spending my afternoons playing ball at the HPER (Health Physical Education and Recreation center) and evenings drinking, like so many of my dorm peers were doing.

Most student managers started with Coach Knight their freshman year on campus. I was one of the few who did not seek the job until my sophomore year. My freshman year had been the Season on the Brink (1985-1986) and my connection with Indiana Basketball was limited to season tickets and going with a cute girl to the games. But I wanted more involvement. Easy to say now, but I could see this was a team with potential and a coach I respected more than anything. I wanted to be associated with them. I wanted to learn to expand my horizons beyond the narrowness with which freshmen see the world. So I worked up enough nerve and called the basketball office as soon as I returned to school in August of my sophomore year at IU.

MaryAnn, Coach Knight's secretary, answered the call. She politely told me to call back in the afternoon in a couple of weeks when the senior managers would be in for training. I thanked her and hung up. Wow, they were already working in August! Today, with all the AAU and travel teams, that would not seem unusual. But in the 1980s I had never been around anyone who played their sport year-round. These were some dedicated folks. Did I really want to spend that much time and work for something that would not be my career path? Two weeks later, I made the call.

To this day, I swear Bill and Mike hired me because I dressed appropriately for a job interview. They may say they hired me because I was over 6' 2" or because they needed more bodies to toughen up Magnus Pelkowski near the rim. But wearing a suit and tie to such an important interview to me seemed appropriate. If only every college student would learn such a lesson that Indiana Basketball reinforced for me.

The first day of practice of the 1986-1987 season was the first day I met Coach Knight. My first impression was not an expected one: he seemed just like my own dad! Whether it was the cut of his gray hair, or the way he held himself, I saw him as I see my own dad. My immediate feeling of shyness was mostly gone. That feeling of seeing a person in a different context served me well not only in my years with Coach Knight, but in life. To be clear, Coach Knight is nothing like my dad. Yet, whenever someone with overpowering strength and force of person makes you question your own internal strength, you should mentally place that person in a different context. Whether it is celebrity status, intellectual superiority, or whatever other reason someone intimidates you, it need not keep you pushed into the corner. To this day, although I am by nature a shy person, I have never been intimidated by anyone for anything. I think many players for Coach Knight learned this or similar lessons over the years. Adversity is not so intimidating if you can put it in a context that you can deal with and handle.

Nothing brings out celebrities like success, and other celebrities. We had more than our fair share of celebrities visit the team during the 1986-1987 season. So many that it became nothing to show up for practice one day and be asked to drive to the airport in Indy to pick up someone whose name everyone knows. Or we would drive to a hotel to pick them up, or simply meet them at the entrance to Assembly Hall and bring them down to the court. People from sports, music, TV, movie, government, military heroes, and those who were celebrities not by their own choice, all came to greet the team, Coach Knight, or both. Naming names is not important, and frankly I do not remember them all. The important point is that every one of us managers learned to handle and deal with celebrities—even more so than the players—so that there will never be another day in my life that I will wait in line to meet someone or get an autograph.

Road to New Orleans

Hoosier Basketball fans are crazy. I never realized how crazy until I was with the team. Fans will wait hours outside doors they think the team or Coach MIGHT walk through, just for a glimpse. Magnify that a hundred-fold when your team is in the Top 5 in the country, and headed to the Final Four. My first year as a student manager and we were headed to the Final Four! After routine wins in the first and second rounds in Indy, we drove the short drive to Cincinnati for a tough regional including Duke and LSU. Thousands of Indiana fans following the team everywhere. Indiana fans are crazy, but incredible.

While in Cincinnati after the Duke win on Friday the LSU game was to be played on Sunday. And as the number one seed we would be wearing the same uniforms. Well, Sunday morning came and we discovered a few of the uniforms had not been washed. Guess who gets assigned to find an open laundromat in downtown Cincinnati on a Sunday morning? Student managers. We always viewed these challenges as fun. This one was stressful. We ventured north of downtown into a not-very-nice neighborhood before finding a laundromat open. With time running out we soon discovered that none of the available dryers were working. Out of time, we had clean but wet uniforms. We had to leave to get back as the team was already boarding the bus to the arena. Tim Garl (team trainer) was anxiously asking us when we would get back. Out of options, let's just say that there was some air drying of team uniforms going on out the window of the rental car as we drove through some of the sketchiest neighborhoods of Cincinnati. People on the street must have thought we were some of those crazy Indiana fans in town—or maybe we were just nuts. The trip to the Cincinnati regional was memorialized that year with a *Sports Illustrated* photo of Coach Knight correcting an error at the scorer's table with an entire row of us student managers in clear view behind him in our red sweaters.

Being a manager gave us the opportunity to travel more than most people do while in college. We traveled via personal car, rental car, conversion van, bus, small jets, commercial airline, and even a few times via private Lear jet. Indiana University had a conversion van that was painted cream and crimson and had Indiana emblazoned on the side. This was the younger managers' frequent method of traveling to NCAA tournament games. And with that paint job there was no denying we represented the university, so we were on our best behavior - other than that speeding ticket an unnamed manager received in Mississippi on the way to New Orleans.

New Orleans did not involve any laundry runs, although there were several trips to electronics stores for more VHS tapes for the coaches as they broke down tape of the teams we would face. We enjoyed the NCAA victory over Syracuse very much. The win over UNLV may have meant almost as much, as it was seen as a victory of pure basketball over glamour basketball, although Indiana had to adapt to accomplish its goal. However there was also a let-down right after the victory in the sense that the celebration shifted immediately to Bloomington, Indiana. Nonetheless, it was a good night in New Orleans with the only instructions from Coach before we left the hotel being, "Remember, you represent Indiana University. The bus leaves for the airport at 7:00 a.m." New Orleans was the pinnacle of a great season for Indiana Basketball and one which I am proud to have been a part.

The Kindness of Coach

The most frequent question I am asked about being a student manager under Coach Knight is, "What is Coach Knight really like?" I never know how to answer that question because I never know what information the person is seeking. I usually answer with the following: Coach Knight is the best coach I have ever seen in any game. He does not act much different in either games or practices than any other good coach or parent I have known in my life—he expects you to do your best and like all leaders he is there to make you better. I have seen coaches who yell more, swear more, get angrier, and yes, are more intense than Coach Knight ever was. None of them ever had the spotlight on them like Coach always did. When things are viewed in a spotlight, they are frequently out of context and certainly out of proportion to what really happened. And what must always be remembered is Coach Knight never said anything to anyone that I would consider a personal attack done to be mean. Criticism of the work you are doing is not personal; it is meant to correct your path and make you better. If you as a player or a manager took it personally, you did not understand Coach's intentions.

One example proves the point more than any other and was one of the most memorable events during a practice while I was there. It was the dark days of early November—the dreary stretch of long practices before we reach the first game—and everyone was getting tired of practices. A player did something wrong in practice, then another player did the same thing. Coach Knight was not happy. He stopped practice and started yelling what they should be doing, all as he walked across the floor with his head down. Often he would act out the movement he wanted them to make. Per usual, when he reached the side of the floor, he would say, "Go again!" A couple of more runs, and the first player had a mental slip and made exactly the same mistake. Coach was beside himself—after all, how many times does he have to say something before a college age adult will understand it and do it? Coach looked angry. He acted angry. As he marched across the floor using the loudest tones possible, he reached the other side where there stood a rack of basketballs. He started picking up the basketballs and pitching his best fastball across the floor.

On the other side of the floor were the two 5 gallon water jugs on a cart that we wheeled out for every practice. Now the water jugs were the bull's eye of the catcher's mitt. Coach had been known to make his point this way before, resulting in a large clean up job for the student managers. I happened to be the manager standing closest to the water jugs. As coach was barking and tossing the first ball, one of the senior managers near me yelled in a whisper, "Protect the water! He's going for the jugs." Holding a ball under one arm, I instinctively stuck out my other hand and snagged the ball mid-flight, just inches from the water jugs. Coach immediately stopped the reprimands, and practice came to a dead quiet stop. Then, in the calmest voice I have ever heard, Coach Knight speaks, "Nice catch son!" Suddenly, there were several laughs and the whole tone of the practice changed. Coach Knight was not attacking anyone personally. He was not attacking the team as a whole. He was not even really angry. He was making his point in his style. A style a lot of coaches use. In the middle of what seemed to be a tirade, he paid a compliment to a person who was not even playing. It was not a tirade, it was teaching. And everyone in Assembly Hall that day learned what Coach Knight was really like.

My senior year with the basketball team was combined with my efforts to apply to law schools. I was pretty sure I had a good enough GPA and LSAT score to get in somewhere, but I wanted to make sure I got into a Top 40 law school. Indiana-Bloomington was top on my list. I knew letters of recommendation were important to the application process. Law schools look for people who show more than just an ability to get an "A" in class. They want people who also have other achievements and efforts in life. Coach Knight agreed to meet with me to discuss writing such a letter. He reviewed my transcript, my LSAT score, then asked where I wanted to apply. I mentioned Indiana-Bloomington plus 3 or 4 other law schools. Coach then displayed a wonderful depth of knowledge of law schools and their relative merits. He told me there was no better school than our own law school at Indiana University. He agreed to write me a letter of recommendation. With Coach Knight's letter, I was confident I had the last piece I needed to be admitted. Those 40 or 50 hour weeks of unpaid work for the basketball team had taught me a lot of life lessons. But ultimately it helped me accomplish a key step in my career goal journey, one that did not involve basketball.

Memories and Moments

I remember the early years as a manager. One of our responsibilities was taping the games. And by taping, this meant going to someone's house in an opposing team's city to literally tape the game on television. This was done in BetaMax format, for those of us that can remember that. Needless to say, the ability to record a game has come pretty far in 30 years.

It was the whole ride for me. The day in and day out experience as part of Indiana Basketball made for a lifetime of memories for me. I met my wife at IU, got a degree in Business and was part of the basketball program. In short, it was the greatest four years of my life.

Mike Agee

✻ ✻ ✻ ✻ ✻ ✻ ✻ ✻ ✻ ✻ ✻ ✻ ✻ ✻ ✻ ✻ ✻ ✻ ✻

One late afternoon, I was sent to the Bloomington Airport to pick up Coach Knight. He was late getting back from a speaking engagement and when he arrived at the airport, practice had already started. I was driving Coach's car (a blue Buick Riviera). When he got in I asked him if he wanted to drive. He said I could, and figuring practice had already started, he would want to get there as quickly as possible. He was napping when we got to the intersection of State Route 46 and College Avenue, when we hit a red light and had to stop. It was the longest red light I have ever had to endure! He looked from under his hat, noticed the light was still red and asked me, "Joe, you're an Education major, right?" I responded affirmatively. "And you want to coach, right?" Again, I responded yes. "Well," he said, "if you can't get a teaching job, you'll never be a wheel man for a bank robber." How do you respond to that?!

My senior year, I was the official scorer at home games. One of the senior managers had that duty in those days. I sat next to Chuck Crabb, our public address and game announcer, and on many occasions he would grab my leg and keep me quiet, since I was supposed to sit there impartially. I was there in that position when referee Jim Bain called the famous technical foul on the Indiana Cheerleaders for delay of game. "Joe, we have a technical on the

IU Cheerleaders." I looked at him with a stunned look. Typically, the famous *William Tell Overture* was played at the eight minute television timeout. But that day it was played too long and too loud and the referee called a technical foul for delay of game. With some "coaching" advice from Coach Knight, that overture was played considerably shorter at future games.

Joe Black

✳ ✳ ✳ ✳ ✳ ✳ ✳ ✳ ✳ ✳ ✳ ✳ ✳ ✳ ✳ ✳ ✳ ✳ ✳

Uwe Blab, former IU player, was one of the smartest members of the team. He would win a game of Monopoly in less than 30 minutes. Most people can play Monopoly for hours and never have a winner.

As an underclassman I spent nearly every day before practice rebounding for Ted Kitchel. Ted is easily the best scorer and most competitive player to be at Indiana while I was there. He could flat out shoot it from anywhere on the floor. I asked him one day, "Of all the places you have been able to play; where is your favorite place to shoot?" He told me, "at home—in my barn."

Ted Kitchel and Randy Wittman were roommates and the best shooters on our team. They used to bet $5 a shot during free throw practice between drills. They didn't bet on makes, they bet on shots made that didn't touch the rim. The difference of who made more determined the winner. Sometimes they would each make 8-10 in a row that did not touch anything but net. In 1982-83 I think they played with the same $10.

Ted Kitchel always got his ankles taped and wore a knee brace on his left knee. During his senior year, he had gotten kicked in the left calf and a game later been kneed in the same thigh. The thigh bruise was painful to walk on so Tim Garl, our trainer, had a sleeve for his calf and protected the thigh bruise by wrapping a football pad around his thigh. He held Ted out of practice the day after the game but wanted him to try and shoot on the end basket to see if the pad was going to stay in place when he moved around on it. Ted's entire left leg is covered in a brace or wrap of some kind.

As is the custom, practice usually starts with the assistant coaches coming out 30-40 minutes before Coach Knight and doing some individual work with each of the players taking up all of the floor space. Ted was sitting on the bleacher near the training room staying out of the way and was talking with Phil Isenbarger, a former player who was now in Law School at IU and a good friend of Ted's. Coach had already been advised that Ted would not be practicing today but when he came out onto the floor from the coach's locker room, he headed straight towards Ted. When he got there he stopped and looked at Ted a second before saying, "You know Kitchel, when Havlicek was at Ohio State he played with two legs that were worse than yours," and he spun around and walked away.

Phil just sat there a minute and said, "You know, two years ago that comment would have really bothered you but not now." Ted looked at Phil, and as straight faced as you can imagine he told Phil, "Havlicek had to play... look who the 6th man was!!" and they both just rolled laughing!!

I was very fortunate to be at Indiana and a part of the basketball. Through Coach Knight's generosity and his reaching out to a kid who had attended his basketball school for 9 consecutive summers, dreamed of being an IU player and who was struggling in school, I was able to transfer to IU in the middle of the year and became a part of the program immediately. My freshman year, 1981, was a banner year as we won the NCAA Championship. As a junior we won the Big Ten Championship and were ranked #1. I was named a Senior Manager in 1984 and like the rest of our managers, was able to help out with the Olympic Team that following summer. I was just in the right place at the right time because of Coach Knight and thus a part of things that others can only dream about. I am a Coach Knight fan and am thankful for his generosity and forever indebted to him for my achieving a college degree. Had it not been for him, I am certain I would not have finished school much less earned a Master's Degree.

While at IU, Assembly Hall was by far the place I enjoyed being the most and learned the most about being successful. The memories, the friendships and the pride that I take in being a small part of IU Basketball mean the world to me. To separate one moment or memory from the other would do neither justice because at Indiana, when you are working for Coach Knight, you know it's a package deal. I am just thankful to everyone there, especially Coach Knight, for making it the greatest 4 years of my life.

Jerry Davis

****

A Special Memory

While I was the head coach at Triton Central, my athletic director made it a practice, in alternating years, to move a home game for the boys and girls teams to Indianapolis and play a game at Market Square Arena or Butler Fieldhouse. He noticed that the Kentucky-Indiana game at the Hoosier Dome was scheduled for December 4 and that we had a game scheduled for the same night. He knew that the floor would already be down and the stadium set up for that game and that if we moved our game with county rival Waldron up a day to Thursday, we might be able to secure the Hoosier Dome. We would still need another game to help defray the cost so I contacted Joe Black (former IU Basketball manager) at Perry Meridian. He had a Friday night game scheduled with Ben Davis that could also be easily moved up.

So I called fellow Senior Basketball Manager and current Stadium Director of the Hoosier Dome Mike Fox to let him know what we were wanting to do. Mike made it all possible and got together with the athletic directors at the 4 schools, the contract and details were worked out quickly, and we were on the books. We had lights, referees, a college length floor and the jumbo-tron at our disposal, but there were no concessions. It was an awesome night for 3 old friends still linked to Indiana Basketball and an Indiana first. These were the first regular season high school basketball games played in the Hoosier Dome and were hosted by manager Mike Fox and coached by Jerry Davis and Joe Black. The three were managers together for 2 years at IU in the early 1980's.

Triton Central and Perry Meridian both lost by 3 points.

Jerry Davis

❋ ❋ ❋ ❋ ❋ ❋ ❋ ❋ ❋ ❋ ❋ ❋ ❋ ❋ ❋ ❋ ❋ ❋ ❋

My Favorite Olympic Trials Story

It was Day One of the 1984 US Olympic Basketball Trials in Bloomington. USA Basketball had assembled 75 of the best college basketball players in the United States. The players had flown into Bloomington that day, taken their physicals and were going to have their first practice session that night. The fieldhouse adjacent to Assembly Hall had been set up to accommodate five basketball courts, and scrimmages were taking place on each court, being run by some of the best coaches in America, including Mike Krzyzewski, Gene Keady and Digger Phelps.

In the middle of the field house was a tower, much like you would see at a football practice, that gave Coach Knight the ability to see all the games at once. After watching the scrimmages for a while, Coach Knight looking none too happy, asked me to go over to one of the courts and tell Michael Jordan that he wanted to see him. It was already clear to all of us that Jordan was going to be the leader of this Olympic team. It was obvious from the very beginning that Coach Knight loved his amazing competitiveness. As Jordan came over to the tower, Coach Knight came down from the tower and stood next to Jordan and began speaking. I was on the other side and could hear what he was saying clearly. Coach Knight told Jordan, "If you think you are going to make this team just because your name is Michael Jordan you've got another thing coming. Now go back to the hotel and if you feel like actually playing tomorrow come back, otherwise, we will get you a plane ticket back to Chapel Hill."

It was not that Jordan was playing poorly; it was Coach Knight's way of setting the tone very early, that there was a certain way this team was going to play and nobody was more important than what that team was trying to accomplish. He knew all the players looked up to Jordan and that they would all get the message. And perhaps most important, he knew Jordan would react the right way.

I can tell you Jordan came back the next day and was like a man possessed. He completely dominated every drill, and every scrimmage the team had the rest of that week. It was a case of Coach Knight doing what he did better than anyone, knowing who he could get on, who needed a pat on the back, what he had to do to each individual to get the best out of them. He knew everyone was different and that they needed to be motivated differently.

While many of those players may not have understood what was going on that first day of the trials in April, a few months later when they were standing on the medal stand in Los Angeles accepting their gold medal, they all understood perfectly.

Chuck Fattore

❊ ❊ ❊ ❊ ❊ ❊ ❊ ❊ ❊ ❊ ❊ ❊ ❊ ❊ ❊ ❊ ❊ ❊ ❊

My Favorite IU Basketball Memories

Typically, our first road trip game at the start of the season was to Notre Dame. In the 1982-83 season, we travelled there on Monday, played Tuesday then returned late to be in class on Wednesday. This season, this was the second road game but the first during the middle of a typical class week. That first practice back was mainly correcting the mistakes from Tuesday. We had won, 68-52. The atmosphere should have been upbeat but the team was tired. During the film session which truly used film, not videotape or digital like today, the team was out of it.

In the game, Coach highlighted a steal by 6 foot 8 inch tall and 250 pounds forward Steve Bouchie, which he made near the top of the key and was followed down court by Tim Kempton of Notre Dame. Kempton was taller and heavier. Steve made the steal then the film cuts to two bull elephants chasing each other on the plains of Africa. The locker room exploded in laughter! It was hilarious! It really lifted the spirits of the team. I am still amazed that Coach was able to get the film staff to splice in that footage. It was a very memorable practical joke.

Coach Knight coached the 1984 Olympic Team. Most of us managers stayed that summer as we couldn't pass on the opportunity. There was tremendous talent on that team, Michael Jordan, Patrick Ewing, Chris Mullin, Steve Alford, Wayman Tisdale, Sam Perkins and several other All Americans. At the time, it was still made up of amateurs from NCAA level players. It was very interesting to watch Coach with those players. I had just spent four years watching him coach with various methods but this was different. Coach molded that talent into a very successful unit in just about four weeks of actual practice. They then went on the road to play some exhibition games, and then went undefeated in Los Angeles, winning the gold medal by an average of twenty points or more.

Coach was impressed with the talent but he truly coached them during that run to the gold. He was more like a horse trainer trying to reign in their talent and ability. He worked them hard but not like his typical practices. He knew that he only had them for a short time so he made the most of it. It was an honor for all to be part of that team.

In January, 1983, we won at Purdue for the first time in my four years at IU. Coach Knight and Coach Crews were going to fly to South Bend after the game to watch Delray Brooks play at my high school, Mishawaka. Delray Brooks was an extreme talent who went on to be an Indiana Mr. Basketball in 1984 (he shared it with Troy Lewis from Anderson). Coach was recruiting him as a junior. Northern Indiana had been hit with snow on Friday and Saturday so their normal ride wasn't able to pick them up from the South Bend airport. Coach Crews asked me to see if someone in my family could pick them up and return them to the airport. My oldest brother, John, jumped at the chance.

After the Purdue game, we are on the bus at the Purdue airport. The team is flying back on the larger plane, Coaches Knight and Crews are flying on a smaller plane. I am on the bus to take us back to Bloomington. Coach Crews sticks his head in the bus and says: "Grab your stuff, Coach wants you to go with us to Mishawaka." Wow! I was returning to my high school with Coach Knight and Coach Crews on a recruiting trip. Coach wanted me to make sure the connections were good. Remember, this was way before cell and smart phones.

My brother was there as expected but he also (unknown to us) brought along my dad, John Gleissner. On the 25 minute plus ride to the game, my dad, brother and Coach Knight discussed baseball, basketball and other sports. My dad was a regional talent scout for Major League baseball in the 1940s, '50s and '60s. My dad also coached, played and officiated basketball over the years. My brother was both a teacher and a coach.

At one point, my dad asks Coach Knight: "What the hell is the matter with John Flowers?" I cringed and uttered: "Dad!" Coach Knight said: "That's okay, Joe. Mr. Gleissner, lately, I have been thinking the same thing. John wants to be a scorer. We want him to set screens, play defense and rebound. We don't see eye to eye on his role." A week later, John Flowers transferred to UNLV.

There is a lot more to the story but that is one of my favorite memories as Coach Knight and my dad shared a great conversation during that ride. I really have appreciated that Coach was very accommodating to my dad. A victory at Purdue helped make that a very memorable trip.

Joe Gleissner

❊ ❊ ❊ ❊ ❊ ❊ ❊ ❊ ❊ ❊ ❊ ❊ ❊ ❊ ❊ ❊ ❊ ❊ ❊

My favorite moment was not just one incident. It was during my senior year (1988) when Assistant Coach Joby Wright asked me if I would be interested in helping with the assistant coaches' recruiting efforts. This job ran for several months and consisted of gathering information, contacting recruits' schools and setting up a calendar of games that recruits played. This gave me the opportunity to work very closely with Coach Wright. I enjoyed doing this very much and I believe it gave me insight into what the future of IU Basketball was going to be.

David Gottlieb

❊ ❊ ❊ ❊ ❊ ❊ ❊ ❊ ❊ ❊ ❊ ❊ ❊ ❊ ❊ ❊ ❊ ❊ ❊

When the team traveled, senior managers received all incoming phone calls for the team. This would prevent players and coaches from being disturbed, and distracted. During my senior year trip to Michigan, I answered the phone. A man who claimed to be Michigan head football coach Bo Schembechler was on the line and he asked to speak to Coach Knight. I thought it was a prank call so I replied, "Sure it is—why don't you talk to Coach Knight tomorrow at Crisler Arena?" At that point, Coach Schembechler raised his voice and replied "Son, if you want to graduate from Indiana, you better get Coach Knight right now!" At that point, I apologized and put him in contact with Coach Knight immediately. At the shoot around practice the next day, Coach took the time to thank me for doing my job and he personally introduced me to the Hall of Fame football coach.

Jim Kelly

❊ ❊ ❊ ❊ ❊ ❊ ❊ ❊ ❊ ❊ ❊ ❊ ❊ ❊ ❊ ❊ ❊ ❊ ❊

My Favorite Memories

As fun as it was to travel with the team, some of the best times we had as student managers were when we could not travel with the team for away games. The number of managers who traveled with the team depended on a number of factors, including the number of seats available on the plane, whether it was close enough to drive, and other logistics. So there were usually a few managers who had to stay home, and seniority prevailed. Our reward for staying home was that we received a game night experience any Hoosier Basketball fan would cherish: we would gather at Assembly Hall to shoot baskets and play ball on the court, order pizza from Mother Bear's, and watch the game in the control room or other fun places in Assembly Hall. I have yet to find a better way to watch an Indiana game.

One of the regular tasks of student managers on game day is hosting the referees for the game. We would prepare their locker room by stocking it with towels, toiletries, ice, water, and candies. This was a job I particularly enjoyed.

First, it was a pleasure to get to know some of the best basketball officials in the country. To a man, they were very friendly and warm with their hosts. Perhaps they knew that if they had a bad game I might be one of the few people able to get them out of the building! We had some very tense games at Indiana while I was there, and there were a couple of time the referees asked that I collect an escort for them out of the building, which I readily accomplished. Actually, I had a couple of Bloomington police officers who worked the stairwell nearby who I could call on if security was felt needed.

Second, the referees were known to tip their hosts on occasion and money was always welcome to a young college kid. However, the best tip I received was non-monetary. One of the first host jobs I did was for an official by the name of Joe Fox (check this). He had just developed a new design in official whistles. These whistles were pea-less, meaning they did not have the little ball inside, but they are louder and at a pitch that is easier to hear. He gave me two of the new whistles as a thank you. I still use them today when I officiate. Now, such whistles are standard usage at all levels.

One of my part-time paying jobs in college was refereeing intramural basketball games. During college I qualified for and obtained my IHSAA certification as a basketball official. Somehow word spread to the Indiana Basketball program that I was a licensed official. Suddenly I was asked to referee scrimmages in practice. Let's just say that refereeing at the college level is several notches above the intramural or high school level. But Coach would take even less nonsense from a manager-referee than he would from a game official. Fortunately, the worst I ever heard from Coach was, "That is not a foul—play on!" Lesson learned.

Nelson Nettles

�֍ �֍ �֍ �֍ ✖ ✖ ✖ ✖ ✖ ✖ ✖ ✖ ✖ ✖ ✖ ✖ ✖ ✖

Favorite IU Basketball Memory

My favorite IU Basketball memory would have to be our 1984 NCAA tournament victory over #1 ranked North Carolina in Atlanta. They had a roster that included Michael Jordan, Sam Perkins, Kenny Smith, and other notable players. At the first practice in the week leading up to that game Coach Knight gathered the team together. He told us that "We aren't going down there to play North Carolina, we are going down there to kick their ass!" He made everyone believe and it proved to be a thrilling game that all IU fans will remember fondly.

Greg Ryan

❀ ❀ ❀ ❀ ❀ ❀ ❀ ❀ ❀ ❀ ❀ ❀ ❀ ❀ ❀ ❀ ❀ ❀ ❀ ❀

My Favorite IU Basketball Moments

I was only a junior at IU but considered it to be an honor to be selected as one of the two head managers for the team, and it was even better that the team ended up winning the National Championship in 1981. Even though circumstances kept me out of the team photo (look at the picture and you'll notice an empty spot on the right), be assured there were two head managers that year. I really don't think much about being left out of the photo until people bring it up and I have to give them an explanation. I loved the experience of the National Championship. The opportunity I had observing the daily preparation, the struggles in Hawaii over Christmas, followed by the run to the Big Ten championship and the incredible display of basketball through the national tournament, leading up to the celebration of the championship. But that is not my top experience during my four years. I am not sure I would place it even in the top five.

Landon Turner and I entered IU at the same time in the fall of 1978. He was a 6'10" Indiana All-Star from Indianapolis Tech and I was a 6'0" student manager from Bloomington South. But I loved Landon and his personality. One of my duties as manager was to hand out a $5.00 per diem to each player when we were on the road. Landon would pick me up by the ankles, turn me upside down in the middle of the hotel hallway and in a joking manner, try to shake more per diem out of me. So when Landon was paralyzed in the summer before our senior year I was stunned as was everyone in the Indiana Basketball family. I didn't know how to react and didn't know what to do or what to say. So basically, I did nothing.

My greatest moment at Indiana was when Landon returned to Assembly Hall for the first time following his accident. I got the honor of pushing him out onto the floor before the game. I remember being in the locker room before the game and I had to use athletic tape to keep his feet from falling off the foot rests of the wheel chair. Those big dogs took a lot of tape! As we left the locker room, we went down a back hallway. I was excited and nervous. I nearly bumped into a number of individuals. Landon just told them to watch out because I didn't have my wheel chair license. We went out on the floor and the crowd cheered for Landon. I parked him at the end of the court under the basket and stood beside him. The reception from everyone in the arena was awesome. I am not sure what it all meant to Landon, but for me, I couldn't think of a more glorious Indiana Basketball moment.

One of our duties as manager was to referee scrimmages. Each year in the fall, Coach held a clinic for high school coaches. During the last part of the clinic the visiting coaches would come to watch practice. These coaches would fill one side of Assembly Hall. (Later, they would be my peers.) Toward the end of practice, Coach yelled, "Let's get some whistles!" That is the manager's cue that the team is set to scrimmage. As the scrimmage moves on, there is a play in which Randy Wittman is guarding the man setting a ball screen. As the dribbler comes off the screen, Randy jumps out and the dribbler runs him over. At the same time Coach Knight yells "That a boy, Randy!" He was acknowledging Randy taking the charge. I blow the whistle and yell "Block!" As the murmur goes through the crowd, and I get ready for the reprimand of the bad call, Coach simply says, "Another call like that, Gary, and we'll get you a job in the Big Ten!"

30 minutes in eight days. That's one half hour out of a possible 192 hours during our trip to play in the Rainbow Classic in Hawaii. Who spends 8 days in Hawaii and spends a total of 30 minutes on the beach? That would be a

student manager for the IU Basketball team during a visit for the Rainbow Classic over the Christmas holidays in 1980. On a long road trip, we did not have an equipment manager so it was up to the managers to do the laundry. So when you practice twice a day before the tournament and then play three games, that ends up being a lot of time in the hotel laundry room.

We ended up losing 2 out of 3 games. After the last game, Coach turned to me and said "You get the earliest flight out of here." With the help of fellow manager Steve Skoronski, we were booked on a flight at 2:30 in the morning. No more sight-seeing. I remember being up 44 hours straight. Who sleeps on the plane after a trip like this? 27 years later, on my 25th wedding anniversary, my wife and I went back to Hawaii, rented a car, and drove to the same hotel. I had my picture taken standing next to the most memorable place from the last time I was in Hawaii, the hotel laundry room.

Gary Sims

✿✿✿✿✿✿✿✿✿✿✿✿✿✿✿✿✿✿✿

During my senior year I had fallen behind in my studies as a result of team travel and other duties related to being an IU Basketball manager. On a gorgeous spring Saturday night I found myself in the IU library playing catch-up in preparation for final exams. As I was leaving the library I walked past the long line of tall windows surrounding the main floor reading room of the library. At 11 p.m. there was one student still hard at work. It was All-American Ray Tolbert. To me, that image or Ray hard at work on a Saturday night when most of campus was enjoying a night out is the epitome of the environment Coach Knight created within Indiana Basketball.

I was very proud to be named co-head manager with my friend and colleague Pete Schroeder in my junior year. One of the responsibilities of the head managers in those days was to be first off the bus to ensure things were prepared as previously arranged. I loved walking into a hotel or arena and stating those words: "I am Dave Skibinski with Indiana Basketball."

Assembly Hall. Madison Square Garden. Every Big Ten University home basketball court. Market Square Arena. Portland Coliseum. And many more.

I got to shoot baskets on some of the most legendary basketball courts in America. Not bad for a guy who got cut from his high school freshman team.

During my years at Indiana services such as Federal Express and devices such as cell phones were not available. And yet, we often had urgent needs that were a call to action for our staff. One such day I walked into the basketball office around 2:30 p.m. after my classes and Coach Knight summoned me into his office. He told me he arranged for us to get an upcoming opponent game film from Ohio State. I grabbed the keys for one of the coaches' cars and headed off to Columbus, Ohio. When I arrived at St. John Arena at Ohio State it was already early evening. The arena was empty as the teams had finished practice and went home. I found the basketball office, but none of the coaches were in the area. I looked around the office but could not find the film. Now then, there was no chance I was returning to Bloomington empty handed. I stood there and thought to myself, how can I contact the coaching staff—then it dawned on me—where would the phone numbers be kept in a handy fashion? I recalled Coach Knight's Administrative Assistant extraordinaire MaryAnn Davis had a pull-out tray on her desk with everyone's phone numbers. I opened the tray on the first desk in the office and sure enough, there was a list of phone numbers. I called Head Coach Eldon Miller at home and told him my predicament and he graciously arranged for me to get the film, amazed that I had driven to Columbus to get the film and was driving straight back so Coach Knight could study the film late that night. Mission accomplished.

Dave Skibinski

❄ ❄ ❄ ❄ ❄ ❄ ❄ ❄ ❄ ❄ ❄ ❄ ❄ ❄ ❄ ❄ ❄ ❄ ❄

My Favorite Memories with IU Basketball

The most enduring is the relationships that I had with my fellow managers, players, coaches, and office assistants. The MOST impressive element about my experience was the level of HIGH QUALITY individuals recruited and associated with the Indiana Basketball program.

Ordering a double shrimp cocktail at team dinners (the standard appetizer for everyone on the team). Didn't want to embarrass myself, so I just ordered along.

In Columbus at the Holiday Inn, sneaking out to change the "Welcome Ski Club," on the marquee to "Welcome Sko Club," in honor of my friend and fellow manager Steve Skoronski.

While playing against Michigan State, Assembly Hall announcer Chuck Crabb announced a field goal made by the Spartans' star player, Magic Johnson. Upon hearing the call, Knight quickly made his way over to the scorer's table, slammed down his fist, and yelled "Damn it, Chuck, his name is Earvin, not Magic!"

During the Big Ten Championship game, NBC announcer Al McGuire was in town to do the broadcast of the Indiana-Ohio State game. I was getting dressed in the manager's locker room when McGuire walked in. I jumped up and introduced myself, and McGuire said "Hey, do me a favor and go out and tell Knight I'm here." I hurried onto the floor where the players were warming up and found Coach Knight and conveyed the message. Deadpan, Knights says, "Go tell him I don't care whether the "F" he's here or not." With that, I dart back to the locker room and deliver the message. McGuire quips, "Yeah, I get it. You go tell him I've got my running gear on and I'm going to work out so I'll be in shape to handle all his "BS" during the weekend." I delivered that message to a grinning Knight.

Best Game: at Iowa, 1980. Michael Woodson just returning from back surgery. Isiah Thomas gets a cut above his eye that Dr. Bomba sews up. Kevin Boyle...tough and nasty. Ronnie Lester...quick as a cat. Great raucous crowd. Extraordinarily tough game that we win. Managers drive from Iowa City back to Bloomington in a snow storm ... at some point our car goes through the median on to the other side of the interstate ... we drive back through the median and on to our side. Our lives are spared. Did I say IU won the game?

Worst Feeling: 1980. Losing in NCAA's to Purdue in Lexington.

Chris Stone

✽✽✽✽✽✽✽✽✽✽✽✽✽✽✽✽✽✽✽

Photo: Courtesy of Dave Skibinski

Trainer Bob Young with Isiah Thomas, Graduate Assistant and former manager Tim Walker, and Assistant Coach Jerry Gimelstob. This photo was taken during a road trip to San Diego—visited the Naval Cemetery in San Diego.

Photo: Indiana University Archives (P0045329)

Class of 1980 senior managers. This image appeared in the home game program for the 1979-1980 season.

INDIANA UNIVERSITY
Department of Intercollegiate Athletics
ASSEMBLY HALL
BLOOMINGTON, INDIANA 47401

TEL. NO. 812—

August 3, 1976

David J. Skibinski
4330 Cameron Avenue
Hammond, Indiana 46327

Dear David:

Thank you for taking the time to write to me and for
sending the information on your past experience as a
manager. Our managerial staff is set up each year by
our two senior managers. If you will stop in my office
at Assembly Hall when you come to school in August, I
will see you are put in touch with them.

Thank you for your interest in our program.

Sincerely,

Bob Knight
Basketball Coach

ls

These letters from Coach Knight are a keepsake for every manager. This is a letter from Coach
Knight to Dave Skibinski with instructions to become a manager.

Steve Skoronski stands in front of the sign in front of the team hotel—the Holiday Inn on Lane Street in Columbus, Ohio. Fellow manager Chris Stone changed the sign from "Columbus Ski Club" to "Columbus Sko Club" in honor of Skoronski's birthday that day.

When the team participated in holiday basketball tournaments everyone on the travel team would often receive a commemorative gift. Here is the participant gift from Far West Classic in 1978.

Photo: Courtesy of Gary Sims

Gary Sims observes practice while Coach Knight speaks with his son Tim.

Photo: Indiana University Archives (P0045330)

The 1982-1983 IU Basketball Managerial Staff. Kneeling (left to right): Mike Agee and Chuck Fattore. Standing: Mike Fox, Jim Kelly, Mark Galenski, Jeff Buckley, Joe Gleissner, Chris Kaiser, Scott Perlson, Bill Himebrook, Jon Jennings, Greg Ryan, Mark Sims, Jerry Davis.

Photo: Indiana University Archives

The 1983-1984 IU Basketball Managerial Staff. Front Row: Mike Fox, Joe Gleissner, and Jerry Davis. Back Row: Jim Kelly, Jeff Stuckey, Chris Kaiser, Greg Ryan, Bill Himebrook, Joe Csenar, Mike McGlothlin, John Jennings, Mark Sims, Jeff Buckley, and Mike Adkins.

Photo: Taken by Tim Knight and provided by Joe Gleissner

Joe Gleissner holds the 1981 NCAA Basketball National Champion trophy following IU winning the title.

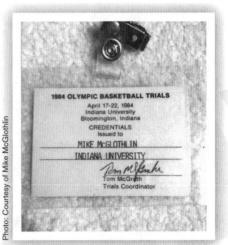

Photo: Courtesy of Mike McGlothlin

Olympic Basketball Trials Staff Credentials

Photo: Courtesy of Steve Skoronski

In 1979 Indiana beat Purdue to win the National Invitation Tournament. Here the team, cheerleaders and fans rejoice following the victory in Madison Square Garden. Steve Risley is in the center of the photo in his IU Warmup jacket, immediately to his left is manager Steve Skoronski, and to his left is team member Phil Isenbarger. Immediately to the right of Risley is manager Dave Skibinski, and to his right is team member Glen Grunwald.

Photo: Courtesy of *Indiana Daily Student*

Coach Knight considered Assembly Hall his classroom, and as with any classroom, you need permission to audit class. Curtains and gates informed visitors to the main floor of Assembly Hall in 1976 that practice was closed. For those who tried to "sneak in" the managers were responsible for escorting them out of the arena.

Photo: Indiana University Archives (P0041022)

Pete Schroeder, seated in the first seat at the scorer's table indicates to the referee that the shooter of upcoming foul shots has a 1-and-1, while Coach Knight indicates he is surprised a foul was even called on an Indiana player.

Classes of
1990-1999

Tim Garl
Head Men's Basketball Trainer
Indiana University

Tim Garl is in his 33rd year as Indiana's men's basketball athletic trainer during the 2013-14 season. Garl is a regular speaker at both national and international sports medicine programs, including numerous presentations in Asia, South America, Europe and most recently at the European Basketball Championships in Spain. He has served at several World University Games including Beijing, Palma De Mallorca Spain, Bangkok, and Izmir Turkey. In the summer he has also worked at the Pan American Games in: Winnipeg Canada, Santo Domingo, Dominican Republic and Rio de Janeiro, Brazil.

A native of Elkhart, Ind., he served as a student athletic trainer (1975-78) for legendary football Coach Paul "Bear" Bryant while completing an undergraduate degree at Alabama. In 1978, Garl was hired at Mississippi, where he served as assistant athletic trainer for all of the Rebels' men's sports. He also completed a master's degree in administration at Ole Miss and completed an MPA degree in Health Systems Management in SPEA at Indiana in 1989.

Garl has worked with numerous United States basketball teams in international competition, including the 1984 gold medal men's Olympic team and the 1982 and 1986 FIBA World Championship teams. He also assisted in the 2002 FIBA World Championships in Indianapolis. Certified by the National Athletic Trainers Association and licensed by the state of Indiana, Garl has served on the United States Olympic Committees and Sports Medicine Committee. He has served since the 1988 Olympics, and was recently reappointed for another four years. He is the longest serving member on this committee.

During the summer of 1996, Garl was appointed chairman of the USOC's Olympic Sports Medicine Society, the alumni group of the USOC Medical Division, becoming the first non-physician to lead that organization. He also serves as a consultant to the U.S. Anti-Doping Agency. Garl was recently selected to the board of directors for the College Athletic Trainers Society. Garl and his wife, Jennifer, have three daughters (Emily, Meg and Haley).

Whatever Was Needed

I have been very fortunate to have been employed by the outstanding basketball program at Indiana University for over 30 plus years. My first nineteen seasons were under the direction of Coach Bob Knight as the Athletic Trainer for Men's Basketball, a position I still hold.

During the Knight years Indiana had a program that was revered by the rest of college athletics. Led by one of the greatest coaches the game will ever see, and supported by the most loyal fans in sports every day was an unbelievable experience.

The system that Coach Knight had developed to undertake the daily pursuit of excellence involved many components. This group consisted of assistant coaches, secretaries, medical personnel, administrative support and a host of others. At the root of this staff was the student manager, the worker bees of basketball. One of my job responsibilities was to supervise these young men.

The position of student manager was one of the most sought after jobs in college basketball. There were dozens of applicants each year for the few open positions. Rarely did anyone ever leave the program, while most sought ways to prolong their stay. Selection of new student managers was the responsibility of the seniors. They knew the expectations of the job and selected only people they believed could do the work and carry on the tradition. The student managers had uncountable responsibilities and worked endless hours. There were few typical days and other than the actual preparation for practice no normal routine. They were on call 24/7 to do whatever was needed by the basketball staff.

They made endless trips to the Indianapolis airport to pick up visiting coaches, guests or dignitaries that constantly visited the basketball program. There were trips to adjacent states where they would accompany an assistant coach and check into a motel to record a game that wasn't on TV locally. Sometimes they drove all night to pick up a scouting video tape, recorded by a supporter, which was needed to prepare for an opponent. There were also the never ending routine errands done for the coaching staff. Late nights, early mornings and occasionally sleeping in the locker room were sometimes necessary to get the job done. All of this while they maintained a full academic class load and progressed toward a degree.

These young men received only token compensation for their work but gained invaluable lessons and had priceless experiences that benefited them far greater than any classroom encounter they had while at Indiana. The exposure and involvement in the behind scenes work needed to maintain a championship program has been considered priceless by most of the participants. The ability to witness the drive and commitment to pursue excellence by a basketball great was something most would have paid for.

There is a tremendous legacy of successful professionals who graduated the program and entered numerous occupations and fields. The ones who entered coaching are well publicized but the others who achieved the highest level of success in non-basketball areas are a true testament to the benefit they received from being involved in the program.

Coach Knight and the entire basketball family at Indiana recognized their commitment and treated them with the highest level of respect. The demands were endless, but their value to the program was always appreciated.

As the last member of the Knight Era staff still employed by Indiana University Basketball, many former student managers continue to reach out to me and remain connected to the program. I hear many stories and relive a lot of unbelievable experiences, but one thing I have never experienced is any one of these men expressing any regrets for the time and sacrifices they gave to the program.

———————

Mike Hall, CFA

Senior Vice President/Investments, Stifel Nicolaus –The Knall/Cohen Group
Indianapolis, Indiana
IU Manager: 1986-1990
Degree Earned: B.S. Accounting, Indiana University, 1990

Mike Hall is Senior Vice President of Investments for Stifel Nicolaus—The Knall/Cohen Group, an investment advisory firm located in Indianapolis, Indiana. Mike's passion is managing and consulting on investments for affluent families, foundations, and endowments. Mike graduated with a Bachelor of Science degree in Accounting from Indiana University in 1990, completed requirements to be awarded the Certified Public Accountant designation in 1993, and became a Chartered Financial Analyst in 1997. Mike lives in Fishers, Indiana, and is the proud parent of two daughters, Ashley (13) and Emily (10).

Be Prepared

I was fortunate to be a student basketball manager at Indiana from 1986 to 1990. During this four year period, Indiana won the NCAA National Championship in 1987 along with a share of the Big Ten Conference Championship. Two years later, the 1989 team won the Big Ten Conference Championship and made it to the Sweet Sixteen of the NCAA tournament.

My last year at Indiana featured a great freshman class that included Greg Graham, Pat Graham, Todd Leary, Chris Reynolds, and future All-American Calbert Cheaney. This talented group would eventually go to the Final Four in 1992. The overall win-loss record while I was a student basketball manager was 94 wins and 33 losses—Indiana won 74% of their games and dominated on Indiana's home court, Assembly Hall, winning almost 90% of the games between 1986 and 1990.

I have been a fan of Indiana Basketball and Bob Knight as far back as I can remember. I watched Indiana's team go undefeated and win the National Championship on TV in 1976. In March 1981, my Dad got four tickets to watch Indiana play St. Joseph's in the NCAA regional tournament. At that time, some tournament games were still held on campus, so my family and I traveled to Bloomington for our first game at Assembly Hall. Our seats were almost at the very top of the arena, but I was thirteen years old and it was incredible just to be at the game watching Isiah Thomas. My affection for Indiana Basketball started at an early age, so when I had the chance to become a student basketball manager in September 1986, I was more than thrilled. I still remember my first day as a basketball manager, standing on the court rebounding for Steve Alford, and thinking what a dream it was to be a part of Indiana Basketball.

It takes a lot of hard work and it is a huge time commitment to be a student basketball manager, but it never really felt like work to me. It was fun getting to spend forty-plus hours a week at Assembly Hall. I developed many close relationships while at Indiana University, and some of my best friends today were also basketball managers. The time spent on the court during practice and traveling to road games built very strong bonds. Besides these valuable friendships, which will be a part of who I am for the rest of my life, I benefited immensely from watching and listening to Coach Knight.

I was a basketball manager, not a player, so it was rare for him to spend much time giving me instructions. But I listened closely. I learned a lot about responsibility, the intensity required to be a champion, the focus on improvement, and the value of teamwork. However, the most important thing I learned from Coach Knight was that success requires preparation. Are you prepared to win? Coach Knight would often say that everybody wants to win, but few have the will to prepare to win.

Coach Knight's preparation for winning was extensive. It included mental and physical preparation of his team. Players were in good physical shape due to pre-season conditioning and demanding in-season practices, where no time was wasted moving from one drill to the next. It was rare for players to line up to run sprints primarily due to the speed at which they had to move during practice. Coach Knight's focus on mental preparation was even more important. He said over and over that "mental-is-to-physical as 4-is-to-1"—the mental aspect being much more important. Every player kept a notebook for scouting reports and to record notes to be mentally ready to play. I believe Coach Knight's will to prepare to win was most evident in the hours he would spend reviewing game film, identifying areas for the team to improve and uncovering a competitor's weakness before tip-off. All student managers will testify that Coach Knight's preparation was endless. More important, as the players took the floor each game, I believe that they felt confident that Coach Knight had prepared them to win. Having "Indiana" across your jersey with Coach Knight on your side meant you were ready to battle.

The last day I spent on the basketball court at Assembly Hall was in April 1990. The basketball season ended after we lost to California in the NCAA tournament and even though my duties as a student manager were over, I continued to study at Assembly Hall. I always felt more comfortable studying there than the library or my apartment. I was about to graduate and was studying for final exams. I decided to take a break and head down to the court to see if anybody was working out. When I got to the court, Chris Reynolds, who had just finished his freshman year, was going through shooting and dribbling drills. Chris was one of my favorite players at Indiana, and he later was involved with the university as Senior Associate Athletic Director. As I was taking my study break and rebounding for Chris, Coach Knight walked onto the court. Coach was very kind to me, and many other student managers, by being a reference as we pursued careers after graduation. Now that my life as a basketball manager was over, Coach Knight asked if I had a job. I told him I had accepted a position with an accounting firm and would start work in a couple of months. As our conversation continued, Coach began to walk off the court and asked "What are you doing at Assembly Hall?" I told him I was taking a break from studying for a very difficult final exam that was making me anxious. Without stopping his stride, Coach said: "If you are prepared, then you have nothing to worry about." It was that simple. Just be prepared.

Over the past twenty-plus years, I have told many people this story about Coach Knight. Everybody is interested about what it was like being a part of Indiana Basketball and being around Coach Knight. It was a lot like that credit card commercial—it was priceless! I am very thankful that I got to spend four years of my life working for Coach Knight and the Indiana Basketball program. Of all of the lessons that I learned, and there were many, the most important one for me was my last interaction with the Coach: "If you are prepared, then you have nothing to worry about."

Thanks, Coach. I always try to be prepared, just like you.

Joe Areddy

Vice President and Senior Foreign Exchange Trader, Fifth Third Bank
Cincinnati, OH
IU Manager: 1988-1992
Degree Earned: B.S., Business Marketing, Indiana University 1992

Joe Areddy began working at Fifth Third Bank after graduation from IU and has been there since. For the past 18 years, Joe's role is foreign exchange trader/advisor. His primary responsibility is to work with companies to help them hedge their foreign currency exposures with a variety of hedging instruments. Joe's territory includes Texas, Tennessee, Indiana and Ohio, as well as managing a team of four foreign exchange advisors in other geographic areas.

Four Years of Work, a Lifetime of Impact

I will never forget my first basketball practice at Assembly Hall. It was October 15th, 1988, the first official day of practice in the college basketball season. Since arriving on campus I had met the players, other managers, and team trainer Tim Garl, but I had not yet met Coach Knight. Being a fresh-faced and wide-eyed freshman, and being one of those Indiana kids who lived and died Indiana Basketball since his diaper days, I was anxious for practice to begin, and equally anxious to see my new boss.

So there I was, standing on the side of the court in my university-issued red shorts and gray shirt, and one of a dozen spare basketballs in arm, thinking I was fairly superfluous to the system at this point (and I was), scouring the court for Coach Knight. Where was he? Would he speak to me? What would he say or ask, and more important, would I be able to respond without vomiting? Senior managers assured the freshman that no, indeed, Coach would not speak to a freshman manager, that if he needed anything, he'd direct the question, or more likely request, to a senior.

As the players were warming up, our practice start time of 3:15 p.m. (and yes, we'd better specify 'p.m.' because of those oft-heard rumors about middle-of-the-night practices) came and went. Then 3:25. Then 3:30. I was thinking that for being an Army guy, Coach Knight sure had an interesting idea of timeliness.

But then, without warning, he was there. He was no more than ten feet from me. Somehow, he had exited his locker room, walked nearly ninety feet across the court, and was bearing down on me without me noticing him. "INSIDE!" he yelled. I jumped. He didn't say it crossly or angrily, but with emphasis and volume so as to be heard and not misunderstood. The players, assistant coaches and a couple of managers went straight to the locker room.

Coach Knight continued past me, practically brushing my shoulders. He was a large man—at 6' 5"—both literally and figuratively. It sounds strange now, after all these years and coming to know him in such a way that he'd eventually just call me "Joe," but at that moment I was truly awestruck.

I checked my pulse and noticed my heart was racing. I felt my forehead and was flushed with warmth. I checked my pants and was relieved to determine that my control of my bowels had not been compromised. And thus began day one, practice one of the best and most life-forming, four-year work experiences of my life.

The first few weeks of practice of the season, particularly my freshman year, were quite frankly not fun. Now that I have kids, I liken it to having newborns. First and foremost, you don't sleep much. Of course, everything is relative, but getting only seven hours of sleep each night seemed like borderline sleep-deprivation.

Secondly, I had very little time for myself. Class, studies, and two-and-a-half hour practices, for which we had to arrive an hour early and often stayed an hour after made for very long days at Assembly Hall. With autumn turning into winter, daylight was minimal. I rarely exited the building before dark.

In short, I wanted to quit. And I almost did. I called my dad in November of 1988 in tears, lamenting that this student manager job wasn't what I expected. He, in no shortage of words, told me I wasn't quitting, and that was that.

So I didn't quit—and I thank my dad regularly for not allowing it. This brings me to another similarity between newborns and that freshman year as a manager. Newborns grow up, and so do freshmen, and so do the responsibilities of basketball managers at IU. The "job" of being manager evolves from mopping floors, wiping down backboards and carrying water bottles into a "career" of breaking down game film, scouting opponents, traveling to away games and making sure road trips are managed without a hitch. The responsibilities become more important and are noticed if forgotten or not handled appropriately.

During my freshman year, there were 19 managers. Most people wonder what the heck we actually did, and why did we need so many. Well, in truth, we didn't need that many. By the time I was a senior, we were down to twelve through attrition and hiring fewer each year. I liked the smaller number because it meant being busier and having more responsibility.

My primary role differed each year. As a freshman, I did many of the "plebe-ish" things—mop floors, fill water bottles, etc. As a sophomore, I usually took statistics during practice. Junior year, I was responsible for writing up the scouting report poster board that was hung in our locker room. My senior year, I booked travel arrangements for our away games. I had plenty to do beyond the above, namely also breaking-down game film, taping practices, participating in drills, etc.

My jobs became more important and more rewarding. And well beyond the job were the friendships I forged, not only with other managers, but with players and coaches, too. My senior year, I picked up Calbert Cheaney from class each Monday, Wednesday, and Friday one semester so that he could be on time to practice—it was too far for him to walk and be on time. I played poker with Alan Henderson and Brian Evans. I went to Red Lobster with Eric Anderson when we couldn't handle another trip to Buffalouie's. I was forging friendships with BMOC's. I was confident and happy and living the college dream. I was growing up and becoming a man, and basketball was a big part of it.

As an IU student, I was earning a degree from a top-flight business school. As a student manager, I was working with a basketball program that was nationally renowned and nationally ranked every year. We competed for Big Ten and National Championships and made the NCAA Tournament each of my four years. And I was working for a man who was arguably the best ever at his job, Coach Knight.

As quickly as Coach Knight walked across the court and startled me four years earlier, my time as a manager came to an abrupt end. My senior year we went to the Final Four. We lost in the National Semifinal to eventual national champion Duke. We led by as much as twelve points in the first half but only by six at halftime. Despite a trio of three-pointers from Todd Leary in the game's final minute, we fell to the Blue Devils, 81-78. Jamal Meeks, my classmate then and Facebook buddy now, missed a three at the buzzer that would have tied it.

Like that, it was over.

I remember the solemnity walking out of the Metrodome that night. I recall getting back to the hotel and Tim Garl asking for volunteers to leave early the next morning. I raised my hand. I wanted to get out of Minnesota and away from the loss that ended my final year of basketball at IU. It was painful.

Later that month—it would have been April 1992—I was interviewing on campus for a job at Fifth Third Bank. Fifth Third would become my employer four months later and still is today. As I sat in the interview room, somewhat nervous, perhaps as nervous as on October 15, 1988, my interviewer, a woman who had graduated from IU, noted that Bob Knight was a reference on my resume. I can remember as if it were yesterday her saying, "Wow, not too many people can put Bob Knight on their resume. Tell me about your experience as a basketball manager." We spent the vast majority of the interview talking about basketball. I got an offer three weeks later.

When I look back at my four years at IU, I am thankful that I earned my degree. I am quite sure that without it I wouldn't be enjoying my relatively successful career. But my role as student manager for Coach Knight and the Indiana Basketball team was by far the most impactful and rewarding part of my four years at Indiana University.

Curt Simic

Teacher and Coach, Bloomington High School North
Bloomington, Indiana

IU Manager: 1989-1993

Degrees Earned: B.S., Recreation, Indiana University 1993
B.S., Kinesiology, Indiana University, 1997

Curt Simic is a teacher and coach at Bloomington High School North in Bloomington, Indiana. His career has included stints at Washington (IN) Catholic High School, where he served as Head Boys' Basketball Coach and Athletic Director, and Bloomington North where he has been an Assistant Athletic Director and member of the coaching staff of both the Boys' and Girls' Basketball programs. In 1997, he was the Varsity Assistant to Coach Tom McKinney as Bloomington North's boys captured Indiana's last single-class state championship. In addition to teaching Physical Education and Health, Curt is also the advisor for Bloomington North's Fellowship of Christian Athletes huddle.

A New Era at Indiana

As October of 1989 approached, the buzz among Hoosier fans was about the freshmen comprising what was possibly the greatest recruiting class in many years. The Hoosiers of 1988-89 had captured the Big Ten Championship on the way to the Sweet Sixteen. Several key players had graduated, but enough remained that, with the addition of a class that included Calbert Cheaney, Chris Reynolds, Greg Graham, Todd Leary, and Pat Graham; the future looked bright.

Throughout the pre-season conditioning process, the newcomers had certainly learned from their teammates the importance of learning quickly. The first day of practice was no exception. As was the custom, there were no lengthy explanations of drills, no walk-through repetitions. The expectation was for you to watch (not just to "see" but to "perceive") and be prepared when your opportunity came. That initial workout likely provided an experience like none the vaunted class of '93 ever had. When it was over, the mental fatigue was certainly on par with the physical.

Coach called everyone to line up on the baseline. After a few brief words, the command came—"Ready—Go shower!" Accounts of the next moments may vary, but one thing is certain. Several players had taken off down the floor in a windsprint—and none of them were upperclassmen. A few may have even reached mid-court before realizing what had been said. Message received. Welcome to Indiana. As Coach would often say, "...and I don't see Clarksville St. Anthony's (or any one of many high schools) on our schedule."

Many other lessons certainly followed. The Hoosiers left the gate quickly, winning all ten non-conference games before ringing in the New Year. Leading up to the Big Ten opener in Columbus versus Coach Knight's alma mater Ohio State, he expressed the familiar sentiment that, although they had done some things well to that point, "...these kids have no idea what this league is about." The learning curve was tough, as Indiana finished 8-10 in conference play before falling in the first round of the NCAA Tournament to California.

The next three years were historic. The Hoosiers went on to win the Big Ten Championship in 1991 and 1993 while reaching the 1992 Final Four in Minneapolis. Included was a 3-1 record against Michigan's "Fab 5." When it was all over, after an NCAA Regional Final loss to Kansas in St. Louis in March of 1993, Coach reflected on the fact that this group had accomplished everything a collegiate team could, except a national championship. ("I wish I could have come up with a better plan to get you there...").

While trying to prioritize the lessons I learned during my time at Indiana, I initially found the list difficult to narrow down. Ultimately, I decided to include those which have become most central to my daily experience today. In order to be effective, these skills must stand on the foundation of solid organization and an ability to work effectively. These prerequisites for success were certainly enhanced during our time in the program. So many of these lessons are common to all of us and, as is the case with lessons well learned, their use is impossible to quantify simply because they are second-nature. I am sure that I am not alone when I find myself having an occasional flashback when something triggers a specific memory of a practice, walk-though, pre-game talk, etc. I also must admit to sometimes hearing specific phrases or teaching points in the specific voice of their originator! I don't believe a day goes by that I don't think about my experience and the way that those four years impacted my professional and personal life.

Any teacher, whether they are just starting out or nearing the end of a long career, will tell you that the ability to break down tasks into teachable parts is crucial to success. The "part-whole" method is as vital to us today as it was to coaches Newell and Knight as they shaped our game. In our constant effort to reach all of our students effectively, we are constantly looking at how to make things as simple and digestible as possible.

In basketball, one of the biggest hurdles can be getting kids to see the value of setting things up in practice that can be directly applied to games. This, of course, was something that Coach really enjoyed doing. In education, the concept and the challenge are the same. Our preparation had better reflect what our goals are. We must constantly ask ourselves relevant questions (What is the purpose of this assignment? What do I expect them to get out of this?). We must give our students practical experience (repetition!) so that they may apply to real situations and learn to make necessary adjustments.

Drill work translates directly into daily practice of fundamental skills. Film breakdown and analysis lends itself to consideration of student data and recognition of individual tendencies. The basic elements of a scouting report certainly apply as teachers try to utilize the "can we" questions in order to challenge our kids to reach higher.

During Coach Knight's A362 (Philosophy of Coaching) class, one of the first statements he made relative to a successful career went something like this: "Your success as a teacher and coach will depend greatly on your ability to demand things of others." This idea applies to anyone who hopes to occupy a position of leadership, but is particularly important to teachers, who by nature have to find ways to address a broad spectrum of learners. An essential element of being effective in this regard is the ability to put yourself in a position to succeed. This cannot be accomplished without knowing both one's own personality and the tendencies and vulnerabilities of the students. In this age of educational reform we are inundated with new means of delivery and analysis, all in the name of increasing student performance. No matter which methods or trends we utilize or follow, the human element remains the link between theory and learning. We must know our own strengths, weaknesses, foibles and flaws and make a constant effort to not only improve but to put ourselves "in a position to be in position." When we apply the same concept toward our students, we begin to make the connection which leads to true success.

When all of the crucial elements have been identified, after you understand yourself, your audience and what you're up against, the link between people is the true test.

One highly effective means of making that final connection is the use of humor. This can obviously mean different things to different people, but it is predicated upon the aforementioned understandings. In the same way that some players or teams do not perceive metaphors, anecdotes or pop-culture references, humor will not necessarily be effective for all students. However, humor can be a bridge to understanding a concept, a personal connection or simply a much-needed break in tension. At the very least, the momentary mood-lightener can provide a valuable diversion. In certain cases, these moments are critical for making other moments possible. Without connection, there often is no commitment. Without commitment, there is no strength or loyalty. Without strength and loyalty, there is no great achievement.

I recall a particular occasion, probably a typical weekend or school-break day, which saw several of us in the "Dup. Room" either breaking down a game tape or editing a game live off of TV. At that time, we had 4 sets down the length of the wall, and all were in use. On the way down the hall, Coach stuck his head in.

Coach (motioning toward one TV): "Who have we got here, boys?"

Manager: "(something like) Wisconsin & Michigan State, Coach."

This process was repeated two more times.

Finally: Coach (referring to the 4th set): "Well, what the h--- do we have here, *I Love Lucy*?"

Prior to coming to IU, I spent a year and a half at the University of California, Davis. While my collegiate playing career was very brief and extremely undistinguished, it showed me that I had a great desire to stay connected with the game, specifically through coaching. My time with Indiana Basketball certainly affirmed that idea. More important than that was my realization that I had acquired some very valuable tools with which I could be successful working with young people in various capacities. It has been said that well-taught players are much easier to motivate. That statement certainly applied to me. While my career in education did not begin until a few years after my days with the program, I did go into the professional world with more confidence and clearer goals.

I consider myself extremely fortunate that I get to work with young people on a daily basis. Being a part of helping someone grow into a successful, productive member of society is the most rewarding thing that I can imagine doing with my life. In that regard, I'd like to think my pride in so many of my former students is similar to the pride that Coach feels toward so many of the men who were a part of his program. I am forever grateful to him for helping me recognize so many things that lead to that pride.

Ryan Carr

Director of Scouting, Indiana Pacers
Indianapolis, Indiana
IU Manager: 1992-1996
Degree Earned: B.S. Kinesiology (Sport Marketing and Management),
        Indiana University, 1996

Ryan Carr is entering his thirteenth season with the Pacers and his fifth as Director of Scouting. Carr will be responsible for overseeing the scouting department. He will also assist Larry Bird and Kevin Pritchard with the team's draft.

Carr, who grew up in Sumner, Wash., served the 2008-09 season as the Assistant Director of Scouting and from 2003-08 served as a scout. After graduating from Indiana University in 1996 with a B.S. in Kinesiology, Carr went to work for the Pacers as a video intern in the basketball department. After one season, he became the video coordinator but left the team in 1999 to become an assistant coach at the University of Texas-El Paso. He returned to the Pacers in 2003.

Carr is married to Kim and they have 8-year-old twins, Caitlin and Austin and 2-year-old, Bryn.

Calm Under Pressure

One of the memories of my years as a manager from 1992-1996 was our trip to Alaska over Thanksgiving in 1995 for The Great Alaska Shootout. We were practicing at a local high school and were setting up to show video in the gym. We had our video projector and VCR on a rolling cart that I was pushing into the gym. The cart wheels hit the door threshold on the floor, and in slow motion the cart tipped forward and the projector landed square on the lens. I quickly put the projector back on the cart, but I had no idea if it would work. I immediately started thinking of other options, but the TV and VCR the school had wouldn't work, as they were old. All of our game tapes were in the Super VHS format, but the TV they had couldn't use a Super VHS input, and the VCR they offered was regular VHS.

I wheeled the cart to the area of the gym we would be watching film, and plugged everything in. I had about two minutes to have it up and running. The projector came on, but I couldn't adjust the focus, as the lens was jammed in the position it was in when it crashed to the floor. I wheeled the cart to a place where the projector was in focus, and although a little bit smaller on the wall from what we normally had, Coach didn't say anything, and a crisis was averted. As much as anything I learned in my four years, problem solving and staying calm under pressure are critical skills. The experience working for Coach Knight was invaluable in preparing me for the rest of my life. Thanks, Coach, for giving me an opportunity to be a part of your program.

Kevin Lemme, M.D.

Orthopaedic Surgeon, FORCE
Shelbyville, IN

IU Manager: 1992-1995

IU Player: 1995-96

Degrees Earned: B.S., Education, Indiana University, 1996
M.S., Biology, IUPUI, 1999
M.D., Medicine, Indiana University, 2003

Dr. Lemme completed his undergraduate degree with a Bachelor of Science in Education at Indiana University in 1996. During his undergraduate years he received an athletic scholarship as a varsity player on the Indiana University Men's Basketball Team. He received his Master of Science from Indiana University-Purdue University at Indianapolis (IUPUI) in 1999 where he also instructed in human anatomy and plant physiology, and tutored students in undergraduate biology. He entered the Indiana University School of Medicine in 1999 and graduated in 2003.

While in Medical School he volunteered at St. Thomas Clinic, worked as an Admission Ambassador Tour Guide, Directed the Indiana University School of Medicine Freshman Review Board, and Co-Chaired for the Indiana University School of Medicine Peer Sponsorship Program.

In 2003, he entered residency at Indiana University Department of Orthopaedic Surgery. During his residency Dr. Lemme attended the AO Trauma Course, the Texas Scottish Rite Orthotics and Prosthetics Course, and the Garceau-Wray Lecture Series. Dr. Lemme is a practicing orthopedic surgeon with Family Orthopaedic and Rehabilitation Center (FORCE) in Shelbyville, Indiana.

Rise to the Occasion

Managers at Indiana University were asked to do much more than fill water bottles and hand out towels. Our responsibilities encompassed a variety of tasks, from the mundane to the highly stressful. The number of managers in any given year ranged from 12 up to 18 during my tenure. At least half of these, on average, were required to have some competitive basketball experience. I was one of these, averaging a modest ten points per game during my final year of high school. The managers would routinely play after the court had been cleaned and practice finished. At that time, assistant coach Dan Dakich would also play with us. We did not set any scoring records but the games were highly contested and it mattered, at least to us, who won.

During the fall of my senior year, Coach Knight hosted his yearly coaching clinic, in which coaches would come from all over the world to watch practices and listen to him speak. It was a three day affair, beginning on a Friday and ending on a Sunday. On Friday, at the first practice, one of the 12 scholarship players went down with an injury. This was a problem because Coach wanted to run three on three at both ends of the court. I was asked by Coach Dakich to substitute in and play. Fortunately for me but not the player, the injury occurred at the beginning of practice. I was then able to play for almost the entire two hours. It was quite difficult, as one may imagine, but I at least held my own during the drills. I was asked to take a seat once the full-court scrimmage began. I was tired but happy that I could help and had fun doing it. The second practice that day progressed much as the first did, with me filling in during drills and sitting out the five on five portion of practice. I left that night pleased that I played so much, encouraged by the fact that my father had been in attendance.

It should also be noted that I had spent the previous summer participating in endurance events like running, biking, and swimming. I even ran two running/biking events and one triathlon. These activities accompanied many summer evenings spent at the HPER playing pick-up games. My stamina was excellent and I was in great physical condition. I was not in "college basketball shape" but I had built a solid foundation.

It became much more interesting, however, the following day when two more players were injured during a rather physical drill. This left us with only nine players. My duties were then extended to play the entire practice, including the scrimmage. We had two practices that day followed by two more the next. It was glorious. By the end of the weekend, I had played more with the team than the previous three years combined. I stuck around after the final practice on Sunday, waiting to talk to Coach Dakich. I offered to keep playing for as long the injured players were out and that I would be happy to do so in order to help the team stay on schedule. He told me that he and Coach Knight had just discussed the same topic and agreed to have me keep playing, at least for the next few weeks. I was thrilled.

I had no aspirations other than what I was currently doing. I was able to play every day with elite athletes and receive coaching from one of college basketball's greatest. Over the next several weeks, I discovered that I was getting the attention from the entire coaching staff, just like the rest of the team. At first it was odd but I just listened and tried to do what was asked of me. Coach Knight would pull me aside and give instruction and criticism like any of the scholarship players. The biggest compliment he could ever give me was just this: he treated me the same. He made me run and do pushups when the team made mistakes. He encouraged me when I made the right pass and got on me when I turned the ball over. I went to bed each night exhausted, beat up, and bruised, but looking forward to the next day. Two bloody noses and multiple floor burns were but a small price to pay for what I was able to experience.

Over the next two weeks, the injured players slowly returned. I made the decision that I was going to keep preparing each day for practice, regardless of whether I was needed. Either one of the coaches or our trainer, Tim Garl, would have to kick me out. I would show up early, perform my managerial duties, and then get taped for practice. My fellow senior managers not only helped alleviate some of the burden of responsibility, but they were also my biggest cheering section. They started to keep track of my statistics during practice along with the players'. Their support was unfailing; one of their own was practicing like a full-fledged team member.

One specific day stands out as a tipping point for future events. Practice was not going well. For whatever reason, no one was playing particularly well, with the exception of Brian Evans who would end up as the Big Ten Player of the Year. Coach Knight grew weary of our poor play and instructed us to start running. We ran up and down for approximately 30 minutes and it was obvious that everyone was dragging. Long distance running and basketball conditioning are two very different matters. Running was easy for me since I had spent all summer training for endurance events. The basketball was what was hard! In their defense, they were not trained for this type of conditioning and I was. We started up play at a certain point and I was refreshed. I scored on a back door lay up and hit a three point jump shot. When this happened, Coach asked us all to leave. Looking back, I think this was pivotal for what happened next. Coach Knight rewarded hard work and mental toughness. It did not matter that I was a manager but that I was able to compete despite the obvious physical discrepancies.

Our first exhibition game was several days later and I recall speaking with my dad and brother about what would happen. I had not been told anything so I planned on showing up in a coat and tie, resigned to the fact that my dream was over. This was not as disappointing as it may appear, once I looked back on the previous few weeks. Being able to play for Indiana was a childhood dream and, briefly, one that was fulfilled, even if the only people that saw me play were in a near empty Assembly Hall. Regardless, my family came down to Bloomington for the game.

The team takes the floor for warm ups 35 minutes prior to tip off without fail. My dad told me later that people were mumbling in the stands around him when this did not happen. There was a delay that would change my life. The players and senior managers were in the locker room dressed and ready to go, stretching out and getting loose. Two minutes until they were to go out, Tim Garl yelled down the hall, "Coach called; get Lemme a uniform!" I was speechless. I stood gaping at everyone; they were all as surprised as me. I took off my jacket and tie and ran upstairs to the equipment room. Our equipment manager had shorts and a full warm up suit ready but no jersey. He asked me what number I wanted and I replied, "Whatever fits!" He tossed me number 23 and I ran to get dressed. I must have looked strange running through the crowd of people dressed up with part of a uniform under my arm. When I returned, Brian put his arm around me and walked me over to the empty locker next to his, telling me that this was mine now. I got dressed as fast as I could and it was very much a blur. However, I will never forget putting on the famous candy striped warm up pants for the first time.

I took the floor with my fellow teammates and went through the drills. I stood in between seven foot Richard Mandeville and six foot 10 inches

Robby Eggers. It was quite comical since I was an inch under six feet with my shoes on. After the game started, I was finally able to catch my breath and attempted to soak in what was happening. I took this as Coach Knight's way of thanking me for the work I had put in by practicing. I was grateful for what he had done and would be proud of being able to help. That was when the unthinkable happened. He turned down to the end of the bench, looked directly at me, and said "Kevin, get Neil (Reed)."

My stat line was certainly forgettable. No one but my family would remember zero points and several turnovers. It was not about the numbers, though. It was about how Coach Knight treats people that work hard, persevere, and take advantage of the opportunities given. He did not stop with just this one game. I dressed every game for the entire season and played in 16. When a player lost his scholarship, he gave it to me. I am forever indebted to him for what he taught me about pushing oneself past perceived limits, whether physical or mental. Both of these I use daily in my life.

One final anecdote will demonstrate how Coach Knight feels about working hard. Against Northwestern, we were leading by a significant margin and I played several minutes near the end of the game. I was the recipient of a back-door pass and scored my first basket as an IU player. It was a fantastic feeling and a dream come true. Upon watching the tape later it was pointed out by my fellow manager, Ryan Carr, to watch Coach Knight's reaction. Usually a stoic man when things were going well, his reaction to my lay-up was a small one: he clapped. Once.

Bob Housel

Firefighter, Indianapolis, IN
IU Manager: 1994-1998
Degree Earned: B.S. Business, Indiana University, 1998

Bob Housel pursued a brief career in business in Chicago and Indianapolis following graduation from Indiana University. In 2001 he entered the family "business" and joined the Indianapolis Fire Department (IFD). This is considered the family trade as both Bob's father and grandfather were members of the IFD. He is now a third generation family firefighter; his family has continuously served the IFD since 1948. Bob and his wife, Amy, have been married for 20 years and have three children, two girls and one boy, whom have all been carefully groomed to be IU Basketball fans.

Prepared for Public Service

My name is Bob Housel and I was a basketball manager from fall of 1994 to spring of 1998. I want to first explain how working as a manager for Coach Knight is still affecting my life 14 years after graduating. I am a firefighter for the Indianapolis Fire Department and have been working for the department for 11 years. What Coach Knight instilled in me has very little to do with my actual job function, but more to do with my overall mindset while at work.

As managers, we all generally had the same type of schedule—2 to 6:30 p.m. on weekdays at Assembly Hall for practices and usually two practices on each weekend day. On game days we were at Assembly Hall early in the afternoon and stayed until well after the games were over which could mean not getting home until after midnight. For away games we traveled the day before the games and usually arrived back in Bloomington in the wee hours following the game. Then add to this the fact that we were students with tests, group projects, papers, reading assignments, etc. But no matter what time practice was scheduled, it was not an option to miss. Whether you had been up all night studying, had been at Kilroy's, or had been waiting for the team to get home after a road game, if there was practice you were expected to be at Assembly Hall.

I won't romanticize my job as a firefighter to make it sound like we face catastrophic emergencies on a daily basis. However, it is not out of the ordinary to get called out four or five times after midnight on a given 24-hour shift. So if we are called out at 1 a.m., 2 a.m., 3:30 a.m., and 4 a.m. it makes for a rough night of sleep. And if we get back to the station after being called out several times throughout the night and the alert tones go off again, then going on the call or not going just isn't an option. You don't stop, no matter what.

My time working for Coach Knight and the team gave me the mentality to respond to these long nights. Back then if Coach Knight called practice; I went. If I had waited for the team to get back to Assembly Hall until 3 in the morning and practice was at 7 a.m., we were there. Today, if I've been awake all night on a fire or various medical calls and the alert tones go off, I go. There is no other option, no matter what.

I am very thankful for the opportunity to have worked for the team and for Coach Knight. It was not easy but, it was most definitely worthwhile. I gave many hours to the team because I love Indiana Basketball. Many of our managers were there to study the intricacies of basketball theory from Coach Knight in hopes of one day coaching their own teams. I was not from that group. I wanted to do whatever I could to help the team in any way possible.

My contribution may have been as simple as filming practices or using the coaches' notes to create a scouting board of our opponents. If helping the team meant driving Larry Richardson to his orthodontist appointment, which I did on more than one occasion, then that's what I did. I may not have ever improved Charlie Miller's shot, but I can say that I rebounded at least a thousand of his shots as he tried to improve his game. And through it all—the good and the bad—I'm still proud of the teams I worked for during my four years at IU.

Joshua Shanklin, M.A.

Upper Elementary Lead Teacher and Clinical Faculty
Xavier University Montessori Lab School
Cincinnati, OH
IU Manager: 1994-1998
Degrees Earned: B.S. Elementary Education, Indiana University, 1998
                   M.A. Montessori Education, Xavier University, 2012

Joshua Shanklin is an Upper Elementary Lead Teacher and Professor at Xavier University. Since graduating from Indiana, Josh has worked as a camp counselor, youth worker, basketball coach, coffee-shop barista, and pastor. Josh, his wife Elizabeth, and two daughters Gracie and EllieAna, live in Cincinnati, OH.

The Shot Clock

Every fall, sometime after midnight madness and before the first game, Coach Knight hosted a weekend Coachs' Clinic. Several thousand basketball coaches traveled to Assembly Hall to watch us practice and listen to Coach Knight preach man-to-man defense and the motion offense. One of the highlights of the clinic, for the attending coaches, was the fact that Coach Knight would wear a wireless microphone during practice, so all that he said could be heard echoing through the Assembly Hall sound system. Ever the entertainer, Coach Knight would invariably make a few jokes at the expense of the players or managers. Our main goal for the weekend was to make sure none of us provided Coach Knight with any material.

It was the Saturday afternoon session of Coach's clinic, during my sophomore year. Practice was about to end, so the players were scrimmaging. I was running the shot clock at the scorer's bench, alongside the court. In an effort to spice things up a bit for the audience, Coach announced that the loser of the scrimmage had to run laps. This provided the spark Coach was looking for, as it caused the players to pick up the intensity and filled the gym with energy.

The scrimmage had wound its way down to the final possession. Rob Eggers tipped the ball away from Andrae Patterson, and gained control of it. As Eggers turned to dribble, he lost control, sending the ball out of bounds and back to Patterson's team. For a brief moment, the ball changed possession, so I reset the shot clock. Coach Knight glanced up to see a fresh 35 seconds glowing from the small clock above the goal. He looked over at me and boomed, "Why did you reset the shot clock?"

I froze. In my mind I knew exactly why I reset the clock. Eggers had possession of the ball, and lost it. There was a change of possession so the shot clock should have been reset.

Coach's laser stare was now locked in directly on me, along with every other set of eyes in the gym. I have yet to encounter another stare as powerful as Coach Knight's. It had the ability to look not just at you, but into you, as if it was probing your very heart and soul for whatever courage may exist there. His stare was an invitation. It dared you. Come on, show me what you've got.

He asked the question again, giving me another chance to defend my actions.

I was replaying the scene in my head. I could see exactly what happened. Eggers had possession. Eggers had possession. But fear left me unable to communicate. The only response I could muster was, "I don't know." His stare found only my cowardice.

"You don't know?" Coach Knight's scowl turned to a grin, his eyes left me, and turned toward the crowd.

"Well, because you don't know, you'll be running laps at the end of practice. As a matter of fact, you just earned laps for all of the managers. I don't know is a terrible reason to do something."

All of Assembly Hall erupted in laughter.

I had shamefully provided Coach Knight with some great material and fully embarrassed myself in front of a humiliatingly large audience. Even more devastating was knowing that my inability to muster up the courage to speak up also led to negative consequences for my manager teammates.

There have been many incredibly large moments in history, where facing down a fear in order to stand up for what is right has greatly impacted the lives of others, the lives of a community, the lives of an entire population of people. A standard of courage is to face those fears. I was not one of them on that autumn day. But that moment left a deep impression on me.

For some, Coach Knight was seen as a person who used intimidation to get his way. I must admit there are days when I felt this was true. But as I reflect on my great shot clock debacle, as well as the rest of my four years at Indiana, I realize that I am thankful for Coach Knight being who he was. I gained from that moment, an understanding of the selfishness of fear and its consequences. I allowed myself to be intimidated, even though I knew the reason for my actions. As a result, others suffered. I was given the gift of an opportunity to learn a lesson, a lesson that continues to shape me, a lesson with ripple effects I will never be able to fully measure.

Thanks for the lesson, Coach.

Joe Pasternack
Assistant Basketball Coach, University of Arizona
Tucson, Arizona
IU Manager: 1995-1999
Degree Earned: B.S., Marketing, Indiana University, 1999

Joe Pasternack has 13 years of coaching and administrative experience. He currently serves as assistant basketball coach at the University of Arizona. Previously he spent four seasons as head coach at the University of New Orleans. While at New Orleans, he quickly rebuilt the program, leading UNO to 19 wins in 2007-08, the school's most since 1997. Prior to UNO, Pasternack spent eight seasons, 2002-07, as an administrator and coach at the University of California, Berkeley. He oversaw the Bears' scouting and game preparation efforts by studying game film, writing scouting reports and helping prepare the team on the court for upcoming opponents. He was also heavily involved in coordinating Cal's recruiting and helped attract several top-25 classes during his tenure. He and his wife, Lindsay, have a son, Joe IV (5), and a daughter, Lilly (8 months).

The Best Three-Credit Class
I was a 10-year-old boy growing up in New Orleans when I discovered my passion for basketball. Despite my dreams of hoop stardom, I realized early

on I would not earn a living as a 5' 8" shooting guard. My goal was to become a college basketball head coach. Fast forward to 1987 and the clincher for me was the moment when Keith Smart hit "THE SHOT" to beat Syracuse in the Superdome for the NCAA Championship. I attended IU for the sole purpose of becoming a manager with the Indiana Basketball program. I was fortunate to have a family friend who was close with Gerry Gimelstob, a former assistant to Coach Knight. With this one connection began the most rewarding experience of my life.

Each day at 3:30 p.m. was the best three-credit class I enrolled in at Indiana as I took notes on the court and in film sessions. Coach Knight and Indiana Basketball provided my most valuable classroom. I was driven to learn the game of basketball from the best teacher / leader in the history of the game. If you want to be a lawyer you go to Harvard, if you want to be a basketball coach you go to Indiana with Coach Knight. He instilled in his players, assistant coaches, trainers and managers a culture of success on and off the court. When you experience that culture for four years, you learn the most important values to succeed in life, in any profession you choose. Today, I attribute my core values to what Coach Knight taught me as a manager, values and life lessons I continue to pass on as a coach and parent. Here are the values that stand out most for me.

Loyalty

The most important lesson I learned from Coach Knight is that loyalty isn't described just in words, but demonstrated in actions. Loyalty is to have each other's backs no matter the circumstances. Here are two of many examples. Landon Turner, a former IU player, was paralyzed in a car accident and Coach Knight took the lead to raise money to defray his medical expenses. As a four-year manager, not even a former player, Coach Knight showed me his sense of loyalty when he convinced Cal Berkeley Coach Ben Braun to give me a chance coaching in Division I. After eight years at Cal, he picked up the phone once again and convinced Jim Miller, Athletic Director at the University of New Orleans, to hire me as a 30-year-old Head Coach. I found myself drawing on Coach Knight's example when I had to make sure my staff and players were taken care of when I left my head coaching post at UNO for an assistant position at Arizona. I feverishly worked the phones to secure coaching positions for my entire staff, and schools for my players.

Prepare to Win

Coach Knight often said, "The war is won before it is even fought," meaning preparation will determine the outcome of the game. His detailed, daily preparations on the court and in film left no stone unturned; he would find any weakness of an opponent and exploit it. On defense, he would find out who we didn't have to guard so his man would be able to help on the post or on dribble penetration. On offense, he would explain if the opponent plays man-to-man, they determine whom they will guard and we determine where they have to guard him.

My second game as UNO's Head Coach was against #21 North Carolina State on national television. They had two 6'9" NBA caliber post players in Brandon Costner and J.J. Hickson. As I was watching game film and scared out of my mind, I said to myself, "How would Coach Knight prepare for this game? Who do we not have to guard? How can we exploit their huge post defenders? The NC State point guard can't shoot! Got it!" Our game plan was developed to double the post with his defender. We also planned to drive against their big guys with our quick forwards just like we did at Indiana against Michigan's Tractor Traylor. Sure enough, the Coach Knight game plan worked and we had the biggest upset in University of New Orleans history that Sunday in November of 2007.

No matter if it was a test in school, a recruiting visit, a game plan, or a presentation in the business world, at IU we learned how to prepare to win.

Discipline

My first team meeting each year as a head coach began simply by putting Coach Knight's definition of Discipline on the board. That was my only team rule. If my kids and players could live by this, what else can a parent or teacher ask?

Do what has to be done

How it has to be done

When it has to be done

As well as it can be done

Do it that way all of the time

IF / THEN

Coach Knight would often say "Basketball is a game of if/then." If the defense plays you one way, then we must counter a different way. Life is about if/then, the consequences we encounter in everyday life. I use this with my son every day. If you do not listen, than the television is taken away; easy to understand and choose to do.

Mental is to the Physical as 4 is to 1

This was one of the most important philosophies frequently stated by Coach Knight. Its meaning is that the mental is four times as important as the physical. This holds true in all walks of life. As we were preparing to play Seton Hall in the RCA Dome he said in a team meeting, "You are here because you have talent, they are here because they have talent. Your mind and your concentration will separate you from them."

Before we played Indiana State, Coach wrote three letters on the board O-W-H. He said that depending upon how we arranged these letters would determine our success that night. We cannot worry about WHO we are playing, we have to concentrate on HOW we play. It is human nature for athletes to let their guard down when they play a lesser name team. Today, as we are preparing our team, no matter if we are playing UC Davis or UCLA, we treat each game the same. As Coach Knight would say, the worst words in the English language are "I wish I would have been ready." We never want to have any regrets.

Master Teacher

Coach Knight's overall teaching philosophy of simplicity and execution meant that progress and improvement would be constant throughout the season if we kept it simple. As the players experienced each situation, they improved their execution. He believed in part/whole teaching. Breaking the offense and defense into progressive drills one-on-one, two-on-two and three-on-three; in this way the players learned the fundamentals of execution. I met with Coach Knight at the Final Four one year and asked him about motion offense. He said "It doesn't matter what offense you run it's how you execute the screening and cutting of the offense. Coach Knight's greatest gift as a teacher was that he demanded exactness every day in practice. He was intolerant of mistakes so his teams would not have slippage in games. I make sure to correct mistakes as they occur each day in practice.

Compete Everyday

In the walk-through room before one of our games with Ohio State, Coach Knight said, "You guys do not understand that the way you perform in athletics is the way you will perform in life. If you do not compete on the basketball floor, you will not compete in life." He was always preparing these young men for life off the court. He created a culture of competition every single day.

My four years from 1995-1999 as a manager under Coach Knight were the best four years of my life. I know that the culture Coach Knight instilled at Indiana prepared me for life as a parent, coach, and any endeavor I pursue. I only wish my son could have the same experience as me when he goes to college.

Jeremiah Shirk

Special Projects Assistant to the Director, American StructurePoint
& Department of Public Works
Indianapolis, Indiana

IU Manager: 1995-1999

Degrees Earned: B.A., Telecommunications, Indiana University, 1999
M.S., Kinesiology, Indiana University, 2009
M.B.A., Ball State University, 2010
Doctoral Candidate, Sport Management,
Indiana University

Jeremiah Shirk is the Special Projects Assistant to the Director of the Department of Public Works for the City of Indianapolis, IN. Prior to working for the City of Indianapolis he served on the executive staff of the 2012 Indianapolis Super Bowl Host Committee in Event Operations as the Manager of Transportation & Logistics.

Before leaving college athletics to pursue advanced degrees, Jeremiah spent the majority of his career in women's basketball as the Director of Basketball Operations for IU, and Assistant Coach/Recruiting Coordinator at Lambuth University. Jeremiah has worked for USA Basketball and started with an internship at ESPN.

Managing Greatness

Former Indiana University Sports Information Director for Football and Men's Basketball (during Coach Knight's final season at Indiana) and friend, Todd Starowitz once asked me in 2002 to describe my first memories of Assembly Hall.

"Prior to enrolling in school at Indiana, I never had the opportunity to visit Assembly Hall despite being a huge fan of IU Basketball, and only living ninety minutes north of Bloomington. One of my first days of school as a freshman I went to sign up to earn the coveted position of basketball manager. At some point I made it around to the southeast corner of the building, which is where the main locker room is, and a door that I would come to use many times. It was the same door I dejectedly sat outside the night Coach Knight was fired.

During my visit, I remember standing outside the locker room, trying to see through the crack in the door. All I could see was the white walls that curved back to the west, red carpet, and Indiana Basketball painted on the wall about half way down. Every fiber of my body wanted to open the door, despite the block letter writing exclaiming—PRIVATE: NO ADMITTANCE—warning me of the dire consequences that might follow if I did. I stood there trying to see movement or something different through my own peep hole for about forty-five minutes to an hour. Finally I got the courage to grab the door handle, and with a gentle pull I found it unlocked, but I didn't dare go in. How could I, a mere freshman, enter this area without permission?

I was in the building for over three hours, yet it didn't seem that long at all. I was in a place I belonged, a place of great importance to me as a seventeen-year-old. And now, at the age of twenty-six, now 35 it's a place of even greater significance because of all of the great things that happened there, but also of equal disdain for all of the troubling things that precipitated the travesty that was Coach Knight's firing. It is a place I can't imagine not being a part of, but never again wanting to fully associate with. The amazing thing about this is that I can still feel everything I felt on that first day: the increased heart rate, the deafening silence of the building, and the sheer excitement of what may happen, what I hoped would happen."

Excitement and gratitude are the two words that describe my time with Indiana Basketball from 1995-1999. That excitement perpetuated from a deep love of the program I grew up admiring from either my parents or Uncle Francis and Aunt Janice's living room depending on whether the games were on the statewide Raycom sports network or if we needed the help of NASA to supply us the signal out of ESPN's Bristol, Connecticut, world headquarters.

Christmas 1996, my sophomore year of college, I was given a license plate from Greg and Carol Hutton of Fishers, Indiana, the parents of one of my closest friends, that read, "Indiana Basketball is not a matter of life or death, it's more important than that." For those of us involved in the Indiana Basketball program during Coach Knight's 29-year tenure, I cannot think of a sentiment that resonates how we felt about the program we gave endless hours of our time, sweat, and ultimately tears on September 10, 2000, at the abrupt end of the program for which we lived or died.

We were often reminded of the honor and privilege we had to serve as managers for the best program in the country when our travels took us to Winston-Salem, North Carolina or Maui, Hawaii, or the comforting, yet architecturally strange confines of Assembly Hall. Opposing coaches and managers were always trying to recon what we did and how we did it in an effort to emulate how we helped our program succeed. I used to respond to the frequent questions of our accountabilities with the following simplistic description, "The coaches coach, the players play, and we do everything in between." If you can imagine it, I guarantee, it at one point, someone on the manager staff did it. We did everything from get water, rebound, set back screens, down screens, flare screens, and cross screens, the staple of the often imitated but never duplicated motion offense that made our teams so difficult to defend. We assisted the coaches with game planning and even participated in practice.

Our involvement in the program intensified in every way as we matured and acquired more responsibility. Through our normal practice duties, Kevin Lemme, who was a senior manager my freshman year ('95-'96), became a staple in practice due to a number of preseason injuries. When it came time for our first game of the year, Coach Knight called Kevin into his locker room, known as "the cave'" located on the southwest corner of Assembly Hall, and told him to get dressed. Don't think we didn't give Kevin grief when he finally moved his personal belongings out of the managers' locker room into the players' locker room. This engrossment permeated our entire operation, from the manager that was awarded the opportunity, to the head manager who had endured 3-to-4 years of work and sacrifice.

Never Accept "No" for an Answer

Throughout my career as a manager I was afforded the opportunity to work on a daily basis with the coaches breaking down film of both our team and our opponents. We spent just as much time dissecting our team on a daily basis as we did each of our 30 opponents over the course of the season.

My sophomore year I was responsible for all of our film exchange. Keep in mind in 1996 we were still using video cassettes that were shipped all around the country via overnight couriers. I recall being at my Grandma Myer's house in Tipton, Indiana for Thanksgiving, because as a sophomore it was not yet my turn to travel. The phone rang and it was Coach Dan Dakich calling from the team hotel in New York City. I had reached out to him because Youngstown State missed the Fed Ex shipping time in order for the videotape to reach my parents' home in rural central Indiana. The beginning of the season and the holidays were always the toughest time of year to obtain film on our opponents, either because it didn't exist, or our trusty Fed Ex wasn't operating. The team was competing in the preseason NIT where ultimately Andre Patterson scored 39 points in the title game to help us defeat Duke. He was named the MVP.

Our subsequent game on the schedule was a short trip to South Bend to face Notre Dame. It was always the responsibility of the assistant coaching staff to have the next opponent scouted and ready to discuss with Coach as the terminating horn sounded of the previous game. I ensured that the Youngstown State coaching staff member responsible for film exchange, was prepared to ship the tape to me at my parents' home the day before Thanksgiving. We had a motto when it came to film exchange to never accept *"No"* for an answer. This attitude was critical to our scouting efforts because while Indiana Basketball was carried on television the majority of the season, our opponents were on significantly less. Of course we had an extensive group of dedicated friends like Bill Freeman and Archie Dees that would help us record games all around the country. If we were really in a pinch we would even solicit the local bars and restaurants like Kilroy's and Yogi's Bar & Grill to record games for us. Our goal was to have a few games for ANY team we might face in the early rounds of the NCAA tournament no matter our seeding, and begin that breakdown the minute our name was called on Selection Sunday. We didn't spend time trying to do our own bracketology; we spent the time making sure we were recording and archiving as many games as possible throughout the season.

I hung up the phone with Coach Dakich with my instructions in hand:

have the Youngstown State vs. Notre Dame tape in hand by the time the team landed in Bloomington following our game the next evening. From my grandmother's kitchen I called Youngstown State, as well as my friends Jeff Freeman and David Johnson, and told them we're hitting the road to Youngstown, Ohio. As with the previous 19 years of my life, I had not missed an IU Basketball game. So, I had to make sure I was back to either my parents' house or in Bloomington in order to watch the game the next evening. A few hours after the turkey was consumed and the kitchen cleaned from our Thanksgiving meal, Jeff, David, and I headed east to Ohio at 1 a.m. so that we could get there, grab the less than 1 lb. piece audio/video magic film encased in hard plastic, and be back in time for a quick nap, watch the game, and meet the team as they arrived back at Assembly Hall. Interestingly this long 350 mile drive for that single game tape was certainly not my last in my career as a manager, or later as a staff member for IU Women's Basketball or Lambuth University.

Always be Prepared

Once my days of film exchange were passed to others, I did more and more scouting, and breakdown of film. Outside of being at practice every day for four years, there is no better way to learn the game of basketball then watching and analyzing hours and hours of game film. My friends always knew during this time if I wasn't in class or home asleep I was likely at Assembly Hall working in the "Dupe Room." The Dupe Room was located in the locker room between team trainer Tim Garl's office and down the hall from the players' locker room. The coaching staff placed an inordinate amount of trust in us as a group of guys that didn't play basketball, and were picked by the senior managers at the time of our application and interview. Annually senior managers screened approximately 50 applicants for the 2 or 3 available spots.

At one point during my junior year Coach was going through film with the team. We were in a stretch of the season when we weren't playing to our potential and I believe Coach was struggling to get through to a couple of our guys. We always had at least one or two managers stationed in the locker room while a film session with the team was happening. The projector and VCR faced the western wall between the entrance to the restroom and showers, while the players' lockers were on the opposite side. The guys sat in front of their lockers, with the name plates of those graduated players of years past like Buckner, May, Thomas, Woodson, Alford, and Cheaney looming over their heads attached to the back wall of each of their red and white painted open-front lockers. The managers stood against the western wall facing Coach and the team as these sessions took place, providing an interesting vantage point to watch facial expressions as time passed. Coach had just spent well over five minutes reviewing a play where Michael Lewis penetrated the top of the key to the right elbow, and pitched to A.J. Guyton on the left wing. A.J. caught Mike's pass and proceeded to pass fake to Luke Recker on the left baseline; that shifted the defense and allowed A.J. to bury a three-point shot at a critical point in the previous game. Luke was too close to the baseline and didn't have an opportunity for a shot, but certainly the opponent knew where he was and was shading toward him. I believe Coach spent the time on this play to accomplish a couple things. (1) To show the guys that basketball is a simple game, which was a mantra of his, and there was no need to complicate things, and, (2) that the smallest, smart play will provide opportunity for success.

Coach had been riding the guys hard the last few days, and I think he was trying to lighten the mood. The next play on the tape was a play where Rob Turner was out of position on defense. To Rob's credit he was so athletic he could've likely made the play wherever he was on the floor, but our system was based on help first, and recover second. Coach said, "Jeremiah, show us where Rob should be on this play." So I walked over to the screen and pointed on the court where Rob should be in relation to his man and the ball. The very next play on the tape, Coach asked me to point where Recker should be. I successfully pointed to the appropriate point on the court and Coach responded with. "Goddamn Jeremiah, that's really good; work on your quickness and we'll get you out there." The team erupted in laughter and Coach shut off the VCR and said, "Let's go outside." Coach is the best I've ever seen at using humor to his advantage as he taught his teams. This was funny to everyone in the room, including myself, because I lived my life with Cerebral Palsy that affects my lower limbs. I was far from being a Division I athlete.

During the four years of my intimate involvement with the program, I made lifelong friends and witnessed great moments that only a select few have. Indiana Basketball gave us tremendous opportunities and developed us into the men we are today. I am forever thankful for the lifelong friends I gained including two people who were an integral part of that family. MaryAnn Davis, Coach Knight's assistant for more than 40 years, has become a dear friend from the day I stepped into the basketball office. Tim Garl, who came on board in the 1980's, has been the rock of stability, and a great mentor to me in my professional career. Not only am I forever indebted to Coach and his family, but I am equally passionate about the friendships made with players, other managers, assistant coaches, and the people like MaryAnn and Tim with whom we worked.

The Team Is Bigger Than Ourselves

The brotherhood of those players and coaches that worked for IU Basketball extends its tentacles all over the world. After I decided to walk away from coaching I wanted to continue my career in athletics. I reached out to Mike Fox, the Executive Director of Lucas Oil Stadium in Indianapolis (also a former manager) about getting an in with the 2012 Indianapolis Super Bowl Host Committee. I had never worked with Mike, but we knew of each other through our association with the program. Because of his recommendation, Allison Melangton, the CEO and President of the Host Committee, and Mel Raines, the Vice President of Event Operations, took a chance, and gave me an opportunity to join the executive staff. The IU Basketball family is alive and well as we all look out for our fellow men, and care for everyone as we did while in the hallowed Hall just north of 17th Street in Bloomington.

Our Impact is Measured After We're Gone

It's not often after walking through the south doors of Assembly Hall my freshman year to today, that I don't get recognized as either a former IU Basketball manager or as a member of the Indianapolis Super Bowl Host Committee. Those two affiliations go hand-in-hand, and make me proud every time it happens. I graduated from the program in 1999 and still get recognized because there were thousands of fans that wanted to experience what we were afforded and thousands of coaches and managers around the world that wanted to learn from the man we learned from each and every day. Indiana Basketball was a program working for championships and striving for perfection. This ideal permeates through each of us, and is what made our program the best in the country for so long.

I still get asked rather frequently what it was like to work for Coach Knight, and I still answer the same, even though my coaching career ended a few years ago. "If I can be half the Coach, and a quarter of the man that he is, then I'll be well on my way." Unfortunately, I don't even believe that compliment does justice to what Coach taught us, and what we are all striving to be.

Thanks, Coach!

———————

Memories and Moments

During my four years at Indiana, three stories stand out for me.

#1: During Coach Knight's tenure at Indiana, our practices were predominantly closed to the public. Anyone who attended practice did so by invitation only. As managers, it was our responsibility to have every person attending a closed practice sign in. The sign-in sheets were typically "stored" on a clipboard. The clipboard typically rested on the scorer's table.

I can count on one hand the number of times Coach Knight actually looked at the sign-in sheet, but on one particular day in November 1988 —yes, about one month after my first practice—he grabbed the clipboard and started perusing the names. I saw him doing so out of the corner of my eye, about ten feet away from me. A few minutes later, I heard, "Joe, why are there only about twenty names on this list and yet about forty people in the stands?" My first thought was, "Why in God's name am I the closest manager to Coach Knight and the lucky recipient of this question?" Since I was not the manager to sign in the guests that day, I didn't really have a good answer.

I froze. I searched for my voice and finally found it after about two seconds (it seemed like an eternity) and said, "I don't know, Coach." There's genius in that answer, don't you think? Before I was able to stick my foot any further down my throat, one of the senior managers, Craig Hartman, came to my rescue. "What's the issue, Coach?" Coach Knight repeated the question to Craig, who looked at the list and accurately pointed out, "That's the list from yesterday, Coach. Here's today's list." And voilà, there were nearly forty names on that second sheet. Needless to say, I felt embarrassed, although I'm not really sure why. It wasn't my fault, right?

#2: My second funny experience occurred during Coach's Clinic weekend, a truly hellacious, two-day event. Each fall, Coach invited a number of high school coaches and friends from around the country to attend two days of tutorials, watching practice, etc. It's a chance for Coach to assimilate with high school coaches for recruiting purposes, as well as instruct those coaches to be better teachers. Our days typically started around 7 a.m. and ended well past dark.

It was the fourth clinic weekend of my career. I was in my senior year and I felt plenty comfortable being one of the managers in charge. On this particular Saturday, Coach was wearing his microphone so the 300 or so attendees could hear him speak. During one of the breaks—and in hindsight, thank God it was during a break so Coach wasn't wearing his microphone—Coach asked me to go upstairs and check on the weather. I have no idea why he wanted to know—perhaps he was going hunting or fishing later that day. I ran upstairs, went outside, took a look up, and returned with my report. "It's a little cloudy and it looks like it could rain, but it isn't right now. It seems to be about 65 degrees. Coach took a minute to digest that answer and looked at me with a wry grin. "Thanks for the detailed weather report, Joe." I smiled. Compared to the sign-in "discussion" three years prior, I could handle the joke about the weather.

#3: My favorite basketball memory is easy to pinpoint, and in fact until we defeated Kentucky in December 2011 on Christian Watford's buzzer-beater, it remained a favorite sports moment in my life.

It was February 19, 1989. We had overcome an awful preconference performance—three losses in December, each time allowing over 100 points, the only time that had ever happened to a Knight-coached team—to be in first place in the Big Ten. That day's opponent was Michigan. The Wolverines were stacked—Glen Rice, Rumeal Robinson, Terry Mills, Loy Vaught, and Sean Higgins, among others. They would eventually go on to win the national title later that year.

Our starting five of Joe Hillman, Lyndon Jones, Jay Edwards, Eric Anderson, and Todd Jadlow wouldn't scare anyone on paper, and until the Big Ten season started, we weren't scaring any opponents on the court either.

But Coach Knight was executing arguably his greatest coaching job ever.

This game was nip and tuck the entire way. With a little over 40 seconds left, Michigan had the ball, up two, and a full 35-second shot clock at its disposal.

We decided not to foul—to play straight-up defense. The implications were obvious: hold them and we have a chance to tie or win at the horn, or give up a bucket late in the shot clock which would seal our fate.

Michigan got the ball to Glen Rice, their best player, low on the right block as the shot clock dipped under ten seconds. He turned, shot a short, eight-foot banker that I'd seen him make countless times, and somehow missed. I was sitting under the opposite basket and from my perspective I don't know how it didn't go in.

Eric Anderson rebounded the miss with five seconds left. He waited, almost too long, for Lyndon Jones to get clear for an outlet pass. The clock ticked to four seconds, then three. Lyndon dribbled up across the timeline and approached the circle with two seconds remaining.

Everyone thought Lyndon would let it fly because there surely wasn't time for him to pass and get a shot off, but that's what he did. He turned left and found his high school teammate, Jay Edwards, who was one of the best pure shooters in college basketball. Jay caught Lyndon's pass and released a shot – quickly—from about 28 feet with the outstretched arm of 6' 8" Sean Higgins in his face.

As the ball arched down to the basket—the one I was sitting under— the horn sounded. SWISH! I raised my arms in jubilation and immediately saw one of the officials, Gary Muncy, indicating the basket was good! It was bedlam!

To this day, that shot is often replayed on various sports commercials and there I am, khaki pants and blue blazer, arms extended, pure ecstasy on my face. It was by far the best singular basketball moment of my managerial career.

Joe Areddy

✽✽✽✽✽✽✽✽✽✽✽✽✽✽✽✽✽✽✽

My favorite IU Basketball memory is an easy one. Watching Keith Smart's shot go through the bottom of the net and being a part of the 1987 National Championship team was a dream come true.

Mike Hall

✻ ✻ ✻ ✻ ✻ ✻ ✻ ✻ ✻ ✻ ✻ ✻ ✻ ✻ ✻ ✻ ✻ ✻ ✻ ✻

A few stories that I remember from my time at IU:

We were practicing just days before a home game with Kansas in the fall of 1994. At the time I believe Kansas was ranked 7th in the nation and our (nation leading) home win streak was still intact. During practice Neil Reed (freshman) brought the ball across half court and promptly had the ball stolen. Coach stopped practice and fired off a classic Coach Knight line - "Neil! Do you have any idea what it's going to be like Saturday? Jacque Vaughn is going to reach down your throat and pull your asshole right out of your mouth!! He's going to turn you completely inside out!!" Side note - we beat Kansas on Saturday by 19 points in one of my favorite games during my years at IU.

In 1998, my senior year, we were in West Lafayette for the game at Purdue. Late in the afternoon I went into Coach Knight's hotel room to start packing up the VCR's and scouting tapes, etc. before going to the arena for the game. Coach Knight and Bob Hammel were in the room talking as I was packing up. Coach said to Bob Hammel, in a low tone that was dripping with disgust, "Can you believe I've spent almost a month of my life in this fucking town?"

My senior year we played in Washington, D.C. in the NCAA tournament and won our first round game. It wasn't unusual for Coach to walk back to the hotel from the arena after games. On this night, Dick Schaap had been a guest of Coach Knight's and walked with him back to the hotel after the game. The managers were in a dining room at the hotel picking over the food that remained after the players had gone to their rooms. Coach Knight arrived and asked for some tape on our next opponent to be taken to his room. About 30 minutes later Dick Schaap arrived at the hotel and came into the dining room that the managers were still hanging-out in. Someone said,

"Hey, Mr. Schaap, weren't you walking with Coach? Why are you coming in so much later?" Mr. Schaap replied, "Well, we were walking back to the hotel together and we came to the Potomac. I had to go find a bridge to get across, but Coach Knight just kept walking—right over the water."

During one of my seasons on the IU campus Billy Raftery was in town to do color commentary on one of our games and he came to our pre-game walk-through. After the walk-through we were talking with Mr. Raftery about various things. One manager said that he was interested in broadcasting and asked for Mr. Raftery's advice on how to make it to the commentator's booth. We were expecting some comment about preparation or paying your dues early before you're given the big jobs, etc. However, Raftery replied, "The easiest way to become a commentator is to first get yourself a job coaching a Division I team. Then get your ass handed to you on a regular basis. Mark my words you'll be in the booth in no time."

Bob Housel

✻✻✻✻✻✻✻✻✻✻✻✻✻✻✻✻✻✻✻

My favorite IU Basketball memory is home game day. I don't have one game that necessarily sticks out in my mind. It is more of a collage of memories and experiences, all of which are associated with home game days.

On home game days, I found it hard to concentrate in class. The anticipatory energy flitting throughout my body was too much of a distraction for my mind to overcome. Not only would I ponder what my responsibilities might be for that night's game, but I would also think through the players' responsibilities. Would we be able to shut down their key players the way Coach planned it? Who was going to be our hot shooter tonight?

Before our appointed time of arrival, another manager and I would head over to the Convenience Mart across the street from Assembly Hall for a sandwich. It was a ritual for the two of us. We had convinced ourselves that eating a deli sub and the little piece of chocolate they wrapped with it would increase our chances of winning that evening.

The journey back to Assembly Hall from the Convenience Mart was probably the closest I have ever come to celebrity. It began with a wave and a free entrance into the parking lot, while others had to stop and pay $20. This was followed by a parking spot right up by the south entrance to Assembly Hall. Next was the good luck hug from the sweet ticket lady. All of this was wonderful. But nothing topped the moment when we were freely allowed to pull open and walk through the set of black doors with the words "No Admittance" stenciled on them. Those doors led to the locker room. Passing through those doors meant you were a special part of a great basketball tradition. Passing through those doors was a feeling that never got old.

Immediately after entering the doors on game day, each of us would have one thing on our mind. What is my job for tonight? The quick walk to the managers' office to see the job sheet was only interrupted by the obligatory shout out to team trainer Tim Garl. While some game day jobs were a little dirtier or more coveted than others, it never really mattered. You had a front row seat for 40 minutes of Big Ten basketball in one of the loudest arenas in the country. It was an honor. Whether it was hosting the other team and meeting their players, helping the Sports Information Director, providing water for the team at time-outs, sitting under the basket to mop the floor, or hosting the officials (please don't let it be Ted Valentine tonight), you were an insider, you were a part of the team, you had a role to play in making tonight happen.

There was no greater moment in all of my time as a manager than coming onto the court with the team during my senior year. As the players ran out onto the court, the band broke into the school song and the crowd erupted. Even though I wasn't wearing the traditional warm-ups of candy-striped pants, it was easy to be convinced that these 17,000 people were cheering for me as well. The energy in the arena would pulse through me. Some nights, if we were playing Purdue, or Michigan State or Illinois, or a ranked opponent, that energy would be so overwhelming, I would become emotional. Five national championships, Coach Knight, Keith Smart hitting the shot, the lady singing the fight song and sweeping as I watched on TV as a kid. This is Indiana Basketball and I was a part of it.

Joshua Shanklin

❊ ❊ ❊ ❊ ❊ ❊ ❊ ❊ ❊ ❊ ❊ ❊ ❊ ❊ ❊ ❊ ❊ ❊

"During the 1995-96 season, Brian Evans was a redshirt senior. He obviously was the leader of our team, and was rarely corrected by Coach Knight. Here's a guy who was around to see the likes of Calbert Cheaney, Greg Graham and Alan Henderson dominate college basketball during the 1992-1993 season. He had been through shoulder injuries and persevered to lead a young and inexperienced team. I was sitting at the stat table, which is now where Don Fischer calls the action on game days. We had a group of four managers that would take stats on just about every category because Coach could ask a question to prove a point at any time. Neil Reed had penetrated the top of the key on the left side, and Brian had just came off a flair screen and drifted to the corner. The defense moved to cut off Neil's drive and Brian dove to the basket along the baseline. Brian's defender had lost sight of him and Neil dished it to Brian moving along the baseline. Most fans will remember that Brian had an awkward looking reverse layup with his 6-foot 8-inch frame and sometimes questionable athleticism. Brian missed the shot and the defense rebounded ending the play. Coach was standing at midcourt facing the swaying NCAA championship banners. As the ball was cleared back to half court and the guys prepared for the next possession Coach said, "Brian, that's not your shot Brian. Brian, in my entire career I've seen one guy hit that shot, Brian. You know who that was Brian?" Silence ... I'm going through the cast of characters in my head; I wonder who he's thinking, Thomas, May, Woodson, Whitman, Graham, Cheaney. Meanwhile Brian didn't answer and Coach let the question sit in the air for what seemed like eternity. Finally, Coach said, "His name was Jordan, Brian."

Aside from the pride I saw in the eyes of my friends and family due to my work with the IU Basketball program, the moment that sticks out in my mind as my favorite was being in attendance in Lubbock, Texas when Coach acquired his 880th win to become the winningest college men's basketball coach of all time. While Coach wasn't concerned with his place in college basketball history, it was significant for me, and I would suspect it meant a great deal too every assistant coach, player, manager, trainer, strength coach, sports information director, and student that was ever associated with Coach Knight's program. At no time in my career was I more proud to be a small part of those wins than in January 2007 in United Spirit Arena, ironically the same building Indiana opened against Texas Tech in November of 1999.

Jeremiah Shirk

❀❀❀❀❀❀❀❀❀❀❀❀❀❀❀❀❀❀❀

Photo: Indiana University Archives (P0021345)

While managers often worked on the court and in drills during practices, it was Kevin Lemme, (here listening to Coach Knight) who earned his way onto the Indiana Basketball Team having started with the program as a manager. Today, Kevin is an orthopedic surgeon.

Photo: Courtesy of Matt Bowen

Shaquille O'Neal with IU managers Walter Muyumba and Matt Bowen during filming of the movie *Blue Chips*.

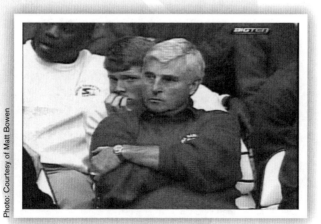

Photo: Courtesy of Matt Bowen

Walter Muyumba and Matt Bowen seated behind Coach Knight.

Photo: Courtesy of Matt Babrick

Here is the scene from Senior Night 1999 at Assembly Hall, Coach Knight's last, standing near the basket are from left to right: Andy Murphy (tan slacks with red vest and white shirt), Matt Babrick, Dusty May, and Kyle Bailey. Standing under the basket are Assistant Coaches Mike Davis, Pat Knight, and John Treloar.

Photo: Courtesy of Don Babrick

Former manager Matt Babrick's father—Don Babrick—hand crafted this replica of Assembly Hall including players and staff from the 1999-2000 season.

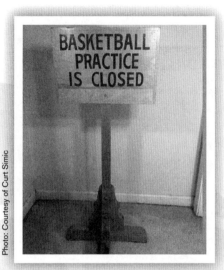

Photo: Courtesy of Curt Simic

A later edition (1992) of the practice is closed sign, now in the personal archives of former manager Curt Simic.

Photo: Courtesy of Dave Skibinski

The plaque awarded to senior managers.

Photo: Courtesy of Curt Simic

Ticket stub from 1992 NCAA Final Four in Minneapolis.

203

INDIANA BASKETBALL QUESTIONNAIRE

Please complete and mail to: **Coach Bob Knight**
Head Basketball Coach
Assembly Hall
Indiana University
Bloomington, IN 47405

PERSONAL INFORMATION

Name _____ Date _____

Home Address _____
                      Street   City   State   Zip

High School _____ Year of High School Graduation _____ Social Security Number _____

Home Telephone Number (AC ____)_____ Height _____ Weight _____

Parent or Guardian _____ Occupation _____

Parents' or Guardian's Address _____
                      Street   City   State   Zip

ATHLETIC INFORMATION

H.S. Coach _____ Office Phone (AC ___) _____ Home Phone (AC ___) _____

Sports Participated In	Position	Avg.	Letters Yrs.	Honors Received
Basketball				
Other				
Other				

Other School Activities (Describe and Indicate Amount of Participation in Each)

SCHOLASTIC INFORMATION

High School Address _____
                      Street   City   State   Zip

Your H.S. Course of Study _____ Educational Objective _____

TO BE COMPLETED BY SCHOOL COUNSELOR. PLEASE DO NOT ATTACH TRANSCRIPT.

SIXTH SEMESTER REPORT   Student Rank in Class—Specify Approx. or Exact
_____ Ranked _____ out of _____ Students _____ Grade Pt. Avg. _____ Out of _____

SEVENTH SEMESTER REPORT   Student Rank in Class—Specify Approx. or Exact
_____ Ranked _____ out of _____ Students _____ Grade Pt. Avg. _____ Out of _____

CEEB (SAT)			ACT (Composite)		PSAT
Date:	Verbal	Math	Date:		V
Date:	Verbal	Math	Date:		M
Date:	Verbal	Math	Date:		Total

INCLUDE DATES OF CANDIDATE'S FUTURE TESTS

I RECOMMEND THE ABOVE NAMED STUDENT: ☐ Enthusiastically ☐ Strongly ☐ Without Enthusiasm ☐ Do Not Recommend

REASON:

_____ _____ _____
Date Completed   Counselor's Name   Counselor's Signature

Recruits were asked to complete this profile sheet to provide Coach Knight and his assistant coaches with all the information they needed to initially evaluate and contact prospective players.

Purdue Game - January 18, 1998

They get their first basket because Guyton stays out with the man instead of positioning himself relative to ball location and gets beat on a back screen, and there is absolutely no need for it to happen if he's in the position on the man that the ball location dictates.

They get their second bucket when Recker goes back to help on the post man and his man cuts to the bucket. Guyton and Gladness are 15 feet out of position to help and, if they are just where they are supposed to be, there is no basket scored.

I think we can do a good job feeding the post against them by taking the ball to the side and then reversing it to a second feeder.

On our first tight cut, the defensive man on the screener steps way out with the cutter and we hit our screener on a slide to the basket.

Gladness gets called for an offensive foul when he sticks his arm and shoulder out and steps into the path of the man he's trying to screen.

Our defense doesn't pay enough attention to where the ball is and what's being done with the ball, and consequently we get caught out of position a lot.

Their third basket is a missed block out by Recker.

The fourth basket they get is a missed block out by Patterson who actually has the guy and then just slides off of him.

We have trouble the entire game getting down the floor to stop their early offense. We can use Guyton up on top moving with the basketball, but we have to have really good movement from the other four guys so we can capitalize on them picking him up.

The way they help on the tight cut, we can run it like down and off the T and take the ball right past the cutter to the post man if the cutter isn't open - the post man being the guy that set the screen for the tight cut.

Gladness gives up a drive to Cardinal's right by being way overshifted to his left hand.

Recker and Turner screw up a straight switch that gives them a three point basket.

On this switch between Recker and Turner, Recker had to do a much better job of alerting Turner to the switch, but then Turner also had to see the switch.

When Guyton, or any one of our guards penetrates, decent things happen to us if the rest of our guys are moving relative to that penetration.

These notes provide a glimpse into the level of detail with which Coach Knight examined his team's performance as he watched film / tape after a game. These are from the game against Purdue—January 19, 1998.

Vashone Rhodes (left photo—dark sweater), Dave Owens (right photo and light sweater) along with Jeremiah Shirk appeared in a Nutrasweet commercial with Coach Knight. A total of 14 managers participated in the commercial; Rhodes, Owens and Shirk played the role as basketball players.

Classes of
2000-2001

Coaching and Sports Administration Roster

Indiana University Basketball has produced a considerable number of players and coaches in the ranks of professional basketball, college basketball and the sports industry in general. The managers that worked for Coach Knight have also established a strong history of working in the world of sports as coaches and administrators. Here is a list of the managers who have spent all or part of their professional careers in the world of sports. We apologize in advance if anyone is left off this list, or any experience has been omitted.

Joe Abunassar
Founder: Impact Basketball, NBA training facility
Founder: IMG Basketball Academy
Assistant Basketball Coach: University of Wyoming

Matt Babrick
Video Coordinator and Scout: Stanford University

Joe "Joe B." Black
Athletic Director: Perry Meridian Middle School, Indianapolis, Indiana
Head Basketball Coach: Perry Meridian Middle School, Indianapolis, Indiana

Matt Bowen
Assistant Basketball Coach: University of Alabama–Birmingham, Valparaiso University
Head Basketball Coach: Bemidji State University, University of Minnesota–Duluth

Jason Buckner

Pacers Sports & Entertainment: Manager of Scouting
IUPUI Jaguars Men's Basketball: Assistant Coach Men's Basketball
2012 Super Bowl Host Committee: Co-Chair Promotions Committee
IMPACT Basketball Academy: Assistant Director, Impact Competitive Training Series
Learfield Sports: Account Executive
University of Louisville: Assistant Director of the Cardinal Athletic Fund

Ryan Carr

Director of Scouting: Indiana Pacers
Assistant Director of Scouting: Indiana Pacers
Scout: Indiana Pacers
Assistant Coach: University of Texas-El Paso
Video Coordinator: Indiana Pacers

George David

Assistant General Manager: Detroit Pistons
Director of Player Personnel: Detroit Pistons
Director of Scouting: Detroit Pistons
Video Coordinator: Detroit Pistons

Jerry Davis

Assistant Basketball Coach: Pampa and South Garland High Schools in Texas
Assistant Basketball Coach: Marion and Hamilton Southeastern High Schools in Indiana
Head Basketball Coach: Triton Central and Wawasee High Schools in Indiana

Scott Dolson

Deputy Director of Athletics: Indiana University
Director: Indiana University Varsity Club

Chuck Fattore
Graduate Assistant Basketball Coach: Indiana University
Assistant Basketball Coach: University of Colorado

Michael Fox
Stadium Director: Lucas Oil Stadium
Stadium Director: RCA Dome
Stadium Director: Hoosier Dome

Lawrence Frank
College Assistant Basketball Coach: Marquette University,
University of Tennessee,
NBA Assistant Basketball Coach: Vancouver Grizzlies,
Boston Celtics, Brooklyn Nets
NBA Head Basketball Coach: New Jersey Nets, Detroit Pistons

Gerry Freitas
Hoop Review Scouting Service
Assistant Basketball Coach: University of Southern California,
St. Mary's, UC Davis, University of Colorado

Jack Gabor
Graduate Assistant Basketball Coach: Indiana University
Head Boys' Basketball Coach: Hammond Bishop Noll, Huntington North,
Kankakee Valley, and Griffith high schools
Head Baseball Coach: Hammond Bishop Noll
Team Camp Director: Valparaiso University Men's Basketball

Chris Giffin
Graduate Assistant: Texas Tech University
Assistant Boys' Basketball Coach: Lawrence North High School
Head Girls' Basketball Coach: Lawrence North High School

Brian Hahn
Head Basketball Coach: Pendleton Heights High School

Craig Hartman
Assistant Basketball Coach: Indiana University

Theo Hodges
Director of Sales & Analytics: Kansas City Royals

Jon Jennings
President and General Manager: Maine Red Claws
Assistant Basketball Coach: Boston Celtics
Video Coordinator: Indiana Pacers

Tom Labadie
Community Affairs Assistant: Atlanta Hawks

John Levenda
Marketing and Ticket Manager: Cal-State Fullerton, Fresno State, San Jose State
Administrator: Class-A California Baseball League
President: Eastern League Class-AA Baseball League

Dusty May
Assistant Basketball Coach: Indiana University, University of Alabama-Birmingham, Louisianna Tech University

Brian Miller
Athletic Director: Hamilton (IN) Junior/Senior High School, Hamilton, IN
Head Track Coach: Hamilton (IN) Junior/Senior High School, Hamilton, IN
Head Cross Country Coach: Hamilton (IN) Junior/Senior High School, Hamilton, IN

Andy Murphy
Video Coordinator: Ohio State University

Dave Owens
Boys Varsity Basketball Coach/Varsity Golf Coach: Owosso Public Schools
Assistant to the Head Men's Basketball Coach: Michigan State University

Joe Pasternack
Assistant Basketball Coach: University of California–Berkeley, University of Arizona
Head Basketball Coach: University of New Orleans

David Pillar
Assistant Basketball Coach: Bloomington (IN) High School North
Referee: 2012 IHSAA Boys' Basketball State Finals
Athletic Director: Jackson Creek Middle School
Official Scorekeeper: IU Men's Basketball (current)

Vashon Rhodes
Owner: Texas Sports Center
Co-Founder: Bob Knight's Field house

Greg Ryan
Graduate Assistant Basketball Coach: University of South Alabama

Mike Schrage
Assistant Basketball Coach: Duke University, Stanford University

Pete Schroeder
Official Scorekeeper: Indiana University Men's Basketball (past)

Jeremiah Shirk

Assistant Women's Basketball Coach: Lambuth University
Video Technician: Indiana University
Support Staff: USA Basketball
Director of Women's Basketball Operations: Indiana University
Director of Video & Information Technologies: Indiana University
Football

Production Intern: ESPN

Curt Simic

Assistant High School Basketball Coach: Bloomington High School
North, Bloomington, IN
Assistant Athletic Director: Bloomington High School North,
Bloomington, IN
Head Basketball Coach: Washington Catholic High School,
Washington, IN

Gary D. Sims

Varsity Girls' Basketball Coach: Edgewood High School, Ellettsville, IN
Head Basketball Coach: Mitchell High School, Mitchell, Indiana
Basketball Coach: Morristown High School, Morristown, Indiana

Dave Skibinski

Assistant Basketball Coach: Army–U.S. Military Academy,
University of Evansville

Jim Stanbrough

AAU Travel Team Basketball Coach

Basketball Coach: Brebeuf Preparatory High School, Indianapolis, IN,
Horizon High School, Scottsdale, AZ, Mesa
Community College, Mesa, AZ

Chuck Swenson
Graduate Assistant Basketball Coach: Indiana University
Assistant Basketball Coach: Indiana University, Army–U.S. Military
Academy, Duke University, Penn State,
University of Michigan
Head Basketball Coach: College of William and Mary

Tim Walker
Assistant Director: IU Varsity Club

Brad Winters
Sports Author

L. J. Wright
Director of Basketball Championships: NCAA

Matthew Babrick, M.B.A.

Vice President, Investment Management Division, Goldman, Sachs & Co.
Los Angeles, CA

IU Manager: 1995-2000

Degrees Earned: B.S. Finance, Indiana University, 2000
M.B.A., University of Southern California, 2007

Matthew is a Vice President in the Investment Management Division of Goldman, Sachs & Co. Prior to joining Goldman, Sachs & Co., Matthew spent four years with Merrill Lynch in its Private Banking & Investment Group Division in San Francisco and Los Angeles managing assets for families and foundations. After receiving his undergraduate degree, Matthew served as a men's basketball scout at Stanford University from 2000-2003. Matthew received a basketball scholarship from Indiana University under legendary basketball coach, Bob Knight. Matthew serves on the board of the ONEXONE Foundation (www.onexone.org) and regional board of the Anti-Defamation League (www.adl.org).

Coach's Core Qualities

I learned a tremendous amount from Coach Knight. Coach led by example, and ingrained certain core qualities in his student-athletes and coaching staff. The lessons and life skills I learned from Coach Knight have shaped the manner in which I live my life and, almost 20 years later, still impact my daily conduct. During my four years on his staff he taught me discipline, time management, loyalty, preparation, and most important, the value of ethics. Below are examples of how I have incorporated and benefited from the qualities and lessons Coach Knight drilled into me as an undergraduate student-athlete.

Discipline

Regardless of the situation or time of day, Coach Knight taught me that the quality of the work I perform is a direct result of the discipline I have contributed to the work output. I have never forgotten his constant mantra of "the mental is to the physical as 4 is to 1." I think of the times I struggled to balance and excel at basketball and schoolwork, and how Coach's words propelled me to success. Coach Knight expected excellence, and nothing less. Under Coach Knight I learned the importance of personal and professional discipline.

Time Management

Working 60 hours a week while on the basketball team and taking a full course of classes at the Kelley School of Business, I had to learn effective time management. There was little room for error and an immense amount of pressure to be efficient. Today, I have adapted the skills I honed at Indiana under Coach Knight to balance my work and family life. Coach Knight instilled in me what it means to be solution-and goal-oriented and that this can only be accomplished through time management.

Loyalty

Coach Knight is loyal to his core. He taught me the value and importance of loyalty in all facets of life. Coach Knight inspired such loyalty and admiration among his players that graduates regularly came back to the program to share their experiences with the current team. While at Indiana from 1995-1999, I learned from several dozen players who shared their wisdom and often acted as mentors for the team. These graduates were examples of how hard work, discipline and loyalty are the pathways to success.

Coach Knight stressed loyalty to the team and to Indiana. In order to remind us that the individual was not more important than the team, Indiana players do not wear their names on uniforms or other attention-seeking garb. Coach Knight would say, "You are playing for the men and women who have two and a half hours of enjoyment watching us play. Give them something to be proud of. You are playing for the front of your jersey, not the back." The contribution a college basketball coach makes to the program and the university is best judged by the quality of its graduates. Coach Knight is responsible for helping to form many successful and loyal men.

Preparation

The words Coach Knight often drilled into us on the basketball court remain motivators for me today. "Failing to prepare is preparing to fail." "Prior Planning Prevents Poor Performance." We went into every game prepared. Typically, Coach Knight would review the prior 10 games of our next opponent and then structure the practices and drills to most effectively prepare. We were expected to be as prepared, mentally and physically, for each practice as if it was game day. Today, I prepare extensively for meetings based on the strong work ethic and detail I learned from watching Coach Knight prepare for each game.

Ethics

Coach Knight taught me that we are each held to the highest ethical standard whether on the court, in class, or in our personal lives. Only with this degree of ethics, can we develop self-confidence, pride and self-worth. Coach Knight graduated players and won National Championships by winning the right way. He did not tolerate cheating or any ethical lapses. Coach Knight taught me not only the value of winning, but also that without values, there is no victory. In an age where the ethics of some of this Country's most successful are being questioned, Coach Knight's lessons on ethics and "winning the right way" are even more important. Coach Knight taught the necessity of high ethical standards in all aspects of one's life, and I strive to hold myself to these same high standards every day.

The older I get, the more I realize how fortunate I was to have had the opportunity to call Bob Knight my mentor and Coach.

David Pillar, Ed.S.

Principal, Jackson Creek Middle School, Monroe County Community School Corporation, Bloomington, IN

IU Manager: 1997-2000

Degrees Earned: B.S. Secondary Social Studies Education, Indiana University, 2001, Ed.S. Education, Indiana Wesleyan University, 2005, Education Specialist/Ed. D., Ball State University, Candidate

David Pillar is currently the principal of Jackson Creek Middle School in Bloomington, Indiana. Upon graduation from Indiana University, he worked as a social studies teacher at Bloomington High School North where he also served on the coaching staff of Indiana High School Basketball Hall of Fame Coach Tom McKinney until McKinney's retirement. In 2007, David moved to Jackson Creek Middle School as Assistant Principal and Athletic Director and later, in 2010, became Principal. In 2012, David refereed the IHSAA Girls' and Boys' State Finals. Since 1999, David has been the official scorekeeper for home IU Men's Basketball games where he has worked alongside Chuck Crabb, Jim Buher, Bill Buher, Carl Harrington, and Kit Klingelhoffer to form the best bench crew in the Big Ten.

"Who's There?"

When you tell people that you were a student manager for IU Basketball and you worked for Coach Knight, everyone asks: "How did you get that job?" We all have a story, and here's mine. Legend has it that the word Hoosier evolved from people in Indiana saying "Who's there?" when there was a knock on their door. Ironically, it was a knock on the door that ultimately led me, a native of Toronto, Ohio, to becoming a Hoosier.

Coach Knight is the son of Carroll Patrick and Hazel Henthorne Knight, who were married in Akron, Ohio and later moved to Orrville, Ohio, where Coach was born in 1940. Hazel's mother was Sadie Montgomery, hence Robert Montgomery Knight. Coach's grandmother Sadie had a brother named Charles Montgomery, who had a granddaughter, Janet Marie Neal Pillar, my mom. So my great-grandfather Charlie is the brother of Coach Knight's grandmother Sadie. (My thanks to family historian Aaron Dodds for ensuring the accuracy of this family history.)

As a senior in high school, I was with my parents, Janet and Bill, at the 1996 Hoosier Classic in Indianapolis. For those of you that don't recall the Hoosier Classic, it was a four team tournament held between Christmas and New Year's at the old Market Square Arena. The Hoosier Classic, along with the Indiana Classic in Bloomington, which was held the first weekend in December, was an opportunity for Coach Knight and IU to bring three teams to Bloomington or Indianapolis with whom either Coach had a relationship with someone at their school, or a school that was in need of a game. The Hoosiers typically beat them mercilessly in front of alumni or people that were home for the holidays.

In the 1996 Hoosier Classic, IU dispatched Colgate University on Friday night, and was gearing up for a thrashing of Valparaiso Saturday evening in the championship game. My parents and I were hanging out in our hotel room at the IUPUI convention center when there was a knock on the door. We were in town with some other family from Ohio, so I jumped up to see who was at the door and found it was Coach Knight. He said, "Hello, David" and, as always, that was followed by, "Where's your Mom?" Coach came in, sat down in the big chair in the room, put his feet up on the bed and talked with my Mom. (My dad and I were smart enough to not say anything until Coach and my Mom were finished catching up.)

When they finished speaking, he turned to me and said, "Have you thought about what you are going to do for college?" Many of my friends were going to Ohio State and I was thinking about that or West Liberty State College, a small D3 school where my dad graduated, now a Division 2 basketball power house. But now I was in a position that thousands of kids dreamed about ... Coach Knight was asking me about college. I was being recruited! I said something along the lines of, "Well Coach, I'm averaging about 10 points and 10-12 rebounds a game." I could dunk and was a decent athlete and was thinking, "Oh yeah, here we go!" Coach then responded, "Well, how are your grades?" (Apparently he was not impressed by my stat line for Coach Mickey Adams' Toronto Red Knights and by this time, as fast as it started, the recruiting process had officially ended). I told Coach Knight that I was doing well and that I was going to finish in the top five of my class. He said, "Well, that's good. Have you thought about coming out to Indiana? I'd set it up where you could be a manager and help the team. I think you'd really enjoy that." I really had no idea what a manager was or did and, although I had been to IU for basketball camp a few years prior, and we had made a few trips to Bloomington to see games; however, actually going to college at IU was somewhat of a pipe dream. My parents were really excited, and I was really excited although I had no idea what I may be getting myself into. We told him we would definitely let him know. Everyone talked a little while longer, Coach left to prepare for the game that evening, and IU beat Valparaiso that night, 72-51.

My parents and I discussed my attending IU and thought it would be a great experience. I then made the decision that would lead me to Bloomington, and to falling in love with a city and university that have been at the center of my life ever since. We made the 380 mile trip to IU for orientation that June. Most freshmen that year, except probably Luke Recker (a new basketball recruit), were herded into groups and walked around campus and then went to fend for themselves with faceless academic advisors they would never see again. I was herded with the others, but when that part was over, I got my own orientation.

I don't think any of us will ever forget our first trip to Assembly Hall. I had been there for camp and for a few games, but this was for real. We met Craig Hartman, who was a grad assistant at the time and our personal tour guide, for my IU Basketball orientation and we met with Coach's secretaries MaryAnn Davis and B.J. McElroy. They promised my Mom they would look after me. They did and still do. Then we went to see Buzz Kurpius. Everyone at IU knows Buzz as the academic advisor to the athletes. I'm still not sure if a nicer, sweeter person exists. After she finished laughing at my score for the Spanish placement test, she steered me to classes with professors like Dr. William Wiggins in African-American Studies and Psychology with the late, great Dr. Bob Weiskopf. Then I was ushered off to WTIU where I spent some time with Keith Klein, who was the station manager at the time. Since I was sure that I was going to be the next Chris Berman, this was a great trip to see how things worked at a television station. Last, we met Tim Garl, one of the IU Basketball trainers. Tim is probably worthy of his own chapter in this book as no one was more important to managers, and in many ways, IU Basketball. Finally, we spent some time with Coach Knight. I was overwhelmed. My mom was scared of the thought of leaving me in Indiana, but all of these people, who truly were the backbone of IU Basketball, are those that have made this program successful and made it a family, eased her fears.

As a manager, you learn the importance of being on time and being respectful, you learn basketball and how to run practices and prepare for games. Perhaps the greatest lesson I learned is that you have to surround yourself with good people, learn from them, and treat them well. Coach Knight did that. I learned this lesson well from Coach Knight and I have used that lesson throughout my personal and professional life. We had great coaches, an incredible support staff, and great opportunities to meet winners. Coach believed in the idea that being around successful people led to learning how to be successful. We practiced with Isiah Thomas, heard from Landon Turner and Bob Hammel regularly, met Tony LaRussa, Jim Thome, Digger Phelps, Robin Ventura, Scott Rolen, and so many others. I used to keep a camera and a baseball in my locker because you never knew who was going to be there. Coach Knight knows everyone! All of these people are winners and have been successful in what they do. Coach shared these friends with all of us so we could see models of winning and success.

There are so many memories from my time at IU. Refereeing practice, trying to guard A.J. Guyton in drills, hiding Swing-In pizzas in file cabinets so we'd actually get one after games, and recording contests live on dual VCR's in the video room long before computer programs and hard drives existed. These were all part of what made my time as an IU Basketball manager unforgettable. Those memories are the ones I will treasure forever. In the end, however, it really is the people.

I think being around Coach Knight and making so many friends during that time is what I look back on most fondly. I wasn't in a fraternity at IU because we were one. The other managers in my class, Brandon Sorrell, Teddy Hodges, Tommy Labadie, and Dan Block, have been friends since we first met. I lived with Tom Geyer and Kyle Hornsby, visited Kirk Haston in Charlotte and New Orleans after he was drafted into the NBA, went to Luke Jimenez's wedding, and catch up with Michael Lewis, Tom Coverdale, and Jarrad Odle whenever they are around Indiana. I keep up with Luke Recker, George Leach, and A.J. Guyton on Facebook, Jared Jeffries on Sports Center, and I still try to teach Dane Fife the 5-second closely guarded rule. I remember hugging A.J. Moye in the locker room in San Diego when we lost to Kent State in the Tourney in 2001, realizing my time with the team was over. I cried when William Gladness and Jason Collier died far before their time. The friendships, the experiences, the excitement, and the heartbreak all were that much more special because of the people that make up IU Basketball. After all, we are family.

My Favorite Memories

#1: One of the great jobs that came from being a manager for Coach Knight was the "airport run." Tim Garl would mosey, yes, he moseyed down to the manager's office with an airport pick-up or drop-off assignment that could be as early as 4:45 a.m., which meant leaving the Hampton Inn on College Avenue at 3:30 a.m., or a pick-up that could be a west coast or international flight that landed near midnight. Who did not have a class, who had access to a car, heck, who had gas, sometimes determined who would go on these 50 mile treks up route I-37.

#2: Just like so many other things from my time working for Coach Knight, I have forgotten probably more than I remember, which is a shame, but I had the chance to make some cool trips. Marques Haynes, a former Harlem Globetrotter who is arguably the best ball handling magician ever, was one of the kindest people you could ever meet. When Marques told stories, you just listened in awe. Coach Al LoBalbo, a former assistant at St. John's, had stories that would leave you in stitches.

#3: The best tipper? Roger Williams, one of Coach's friends is a former Secretary of State for the State of Texas wins that award hands down. One year, Roger brought a group of friends that included former TCU and New York Jets linebacker Kyle Clifton to a ball game. They had a 6 a.m. flight back to Dallas the next morning. Roger knew the 3:30 a.m. departure time was not in the normal routine of a college sophomore and he acknowledged it with a tip that covered my rent for about two months!

#4: Since 1999, I have been very fortunate to have the best seat in Assembly Hall. I sit next to Chuck Crabb and wear the stripes as I serve as the official scorekeeper for home games. Over the years, I have seen some amazing shots like Kirk Haston and Lynn Washington in consecutive years over Michigan State, some heartbreakers like the infamous UNC-Charlotte game where the ESPN truck clock wasn't synched with the Assembly Hall clock. However, after seeing tremendous ups and downs over the last fifteen years, witnessing Christian Watford's three-pointer against Kentucky in December of 2011 was an unforgettable moment that meant Indiana Basketball, the program, was back. Many of us have been here for the ups and downs and that game, that shot, validated the hard work and sacrifice that many put in over the last challenging decade.

David Pillar

❊❊❊❊❊❊❊❊❊❊❊❊❊❊❊❊❊❊❊